# ESSENTIAL *TENNIS*

ESSEN

# IAL
# TENNIS

## A PLAYER'S GUIDE

### Scott Perlstein

EDITED BY
JOANNE McCONNELL

LYONS & BURFORD, PUBLISHERS

Printed in the United States of America

Design by MRP

10 9 8 7 6 5 4 3

Photos by Mark Perlstein. Pictured: Karen Woodell Perlstein, Joe Cammarata,
Charlie Cammarata, Danny Ganoza, Irwin Tu, Dave Luther, Reg Drew, and Scott
Perlstein.

Library of Congress Cataloging-in-Publication Data

Perlstein, Scott.
    Essential tennis: a player's guide/by Scott Perlstein; edited by Joanne
McConnell.
        p.    cm.
    Includes index.
    ISBN 1-55821-220-5
        1. Tennis.   I. McConnell, Joanne.   II. Title.
    GV995.P396 1993                                                          93-453
    796.342 — dc20                                                              CIP

*This book is dedicated to numerous people who have inspired my tennis and been instrumental in organizing the materials presented:*

*First and foremost to my wife Karen for helping me*
*   continue to grow as a player and coach;*
*My father, who was my first coach;*
*J. Cary Bachman, my high school coach;*
*Jeff Unger, my main mentor in tennis during my youth;*
*Greg Sheppard, my main California tennis mentor;*
*Tim Gullikson, for the opportunity to coach at the pro level;*
*Joan Johnson, who first helped compile this material;*
*Joanne McConnell, who compiled the finished product; and*
*My clients, who inspire me to always be inventive.*

# CONTENTS

# FOREWORD

Tennis has been a part of my life for a long time, but my background in tennis is somewhat unusual. Most touring tennis pros began their specialization in tennis at a very early age, often attending one of the tennis academies or participating in a major college program. In contrast, I — along with my twin brother, Tom — played a variety of sports in high school and college. I played baseball, basketball, and tennis in high school and basketball and tennis in college. After graduating from Northern Illinois University, I taught tennis at the Kettering Tennis Center for almost two years before embarking on my professional career. And I chose tennis as a career because I believed that it offered me the best opportunity for long-term involvement in sports.

During my 12-year playing career, I was in over 40 Grand Prix finals and won 16 doubles and 4 singles titles. I have played and beaten some of the biggest names in tennis, including Bjorn Borg and John McEnroe. When my playing days came to an end, I again chose tennis as a career and began coaching the pros in 1986. I have worked with such well-known players as Martina Navratilova, Mary Jo Fernandez, and Pete Sampras. I am coaching today because I enjoy the one-on-one relationship between player and coach. Each client is different and presents a new challenge. This more diverse experience and later start have given me a unique perspective on the strategies of sports in general and tennis in particular.

I tell you all this to help you understand that my background makes me especially qualified to comment on this book by my friend Scott Perlstein — or, as I have always called him, "Perl." Perl and I go back a long way. In 1967, when Tom and I were the Wisconsin state high school doubles champions, Perl was the singles champion. Today, there is no one in the tennis-teaching business who is a match for him. He has greater enthusiasm, works harder, and spends more hours teaching every week than anyone I have ever met. I marvel at the wide range of talent the Perl works with. One of the many philosophies we share is that you are never finished learning about the game; there is always more growth to achieve. The game of tennis is always evolving, and new players and equipment add to the game yearly. Another philosophy we share is that instructors have to keep playing themselves to stay in touch with the game. Both Perl and I continue to play seniors tournaments, and we both believe that we are beating back the aging process.

This book reflects Perl's enthusiasm and commitment to growth and learning. The concepts presented cut across all aspects of the game — the rules, the equipment, the techniques, the strategies, the mistakes, and the mental processes involved. This book is your ticket to a total understanding of tennis and will take your game to unlimited heights.

— TIM GULLIKSON

# INTRODUCTION

## WHY TENNIS?

Tennis is a great game. Playing tennis regularly adds to your health and fitness by increasing your aerobic capacity, decreasing your body fat, and improving your reaction time. Tennis is not just a game of sport, but a game of life. In order to be successful in tennis, you need excellent life skills as well as excellent tennis skills. Tennis players must mentally prepare for the coming battle, develop a battle plan, and have the courage to see that plan through, with enough flexibility to make adjustments as the advantage changes hands.

The most important element of tennis is to always be a student of the game. No matter how knowledgeable or experienced a player is, there is always more to be learned, always another new player on the horizon who will add a new dimension to the game. Even the players at the highest level of the sport continually seek more input and knowledge.

Why choose tennis over other sports? First and foremost, because tennis is a sport for life. A person may be too old or too young to start most sports, but not tennis. The late actor Edward Everett

Horton played tennis into his nineties. Although a person may participate in many team activities in youth, by adulthood these group activities have usually fallen by the wayside as career and family obligations take hold. But tennis requires only one other person.

Tennis is also a sport that can be played by people of all body types and sizes. A player doesn't need to be 6'8" as in basketball, or weigh over 200 pounds as in many football positions. It is not necessary or even a great advantage to be large or tall.

Tennis is a sport of equal opportunity. At the Australian Open and the U.S. Open, the prize money for men and women is equal. In the United States, most high schools and colleges provide women's as well as men's tennis programs.

One of the many wonderful aspects of tennis is its tier system. There are many players at each level of ability to welcome a new opponent.

## Why a Player's Handbook?

Most tennis players don't have a clue about how to play tennis. This handbook gives you the information needed to be a serious student of the game: the shots, the strategies, the drills needed to become an expert and knowledgeable tennis player. In tennis, the more the player knows, the greater the success. As your knowledge and skill level grow, so will your confidence.

I teach fifty-eight hours of tennis every week. Since the waiting list to become one of my pupils is over two years now, I've written this players guide to reach those of you I can't teach personally. Although no book can replace the instructor/pupil relationship, this book was designed as a shortcut for the serious student. You will receive a lifetime of information that will not only improve your skill level but also increase your enjoyment of the game, whether you are a beginner or a touring pro. Although not every player gets to be a world champion, being out there and participating is what the game is all about.

# ONE

# BASIC RULES OF THE GAME

**B**efore beginning any new sport, a player should learn the basic rules and expected conduct. Tennis is played on a court that is 78 feet long and divided horizontally by a net in the middle. Thus each side has 39 feet of hitting length. The singles court, used when each side has only one player, is 27 feet wide. The doubles court, with two players to a side, expands 4.5 feet on each side to 36 feet. The net is 3 feet high in the middle of the court; 3.5 feet on the sidelines.

## CHOOSING SIDES

To determine who serves, the pros flip a coin. Everyone else spins a racquet. Each racquet has a distinctive up and down side. For instance, the grip handle of a Wilson racquet has a *W* on it, so a player calls either *M* or *W*. The winner of this spin can choose to serve or return, or can choose a side and place the burden of deciding to serve or receive on the opponent.

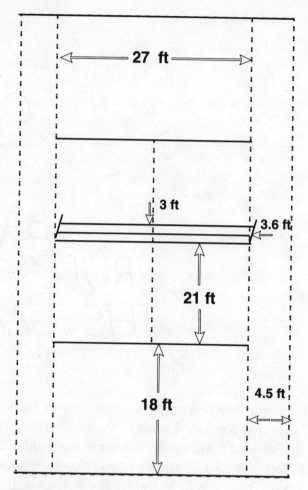

The tennis court

Many players like to receive the first game because it gives them one game to get into the match. Most big servers prefer to start serving because they believe that it gives them the psychological advantage and keeps them on the offensive. One reason for choosing one side over the other would be to hit with the wind rather than into it for two of the first three games or not to serve into the sun on your first service game.

## SCORING

Tennis matches are played in *sets*. To win a set, one player must win at least six games by a margin of two. Thus the score can be 6–0 through 6–4, but not 6–5, which would require one more game to be played. If the score becomes 7–5, the set is over, but if the set becomes tied at 6–6, a tiebreaker is played (more on this later).

Most *matches* consist of a two-out-of-three-set format, except in the Grand Slam, Davis Cup events, and a few other pro tournaments, where the men play matches based on winning three out of five sets. The only women's event to use the three-out-of-five-set format is the culmination tournament of the tour.

There are two ways to score a single *game* of tennis: no ad and regular scoring. In the no-ad (short for no advantage) format, the first player to win four points wins the game. Thus when the score is 3–3, only one more point is played, and the receiver decides to which side the server must serve. Many tournaments use this scoring method to move the sets along. No ad is also a good scoring method when court time is limited.

In the regular scoring method, one player must still win four points, but by a margin of two. Zero points is called love; one point is called 15; two points, 30; three points 40. After 40–40, called *deuce*, there are no more numbers. At deuce, both players are two points away from winning the game. If the server wins the deuce point, this is called *advantage in*, meaning that the server needs just one more point to win. If the receiver wins the deuce point, it's *advantage out*, meaning that the receiver needs just one more point to win. If the receiver loses the next point, however, the score is tied again at deuce. This continues until one player wins both the deuce point and the following point (the *ad point*). *Points* are scored by hitting a winning shot or by the opponent missing a shot.

The serving square in which the deuce point is played is often referred to as the *deuce court*. The serving square in which the ad point is played is called the *ad court*.

*Holding serve* means that the server has won the game—the serve was held. *Breaking serve* means that the opponent has won the server's game.

Some players use slang terminology in scoring. Fifteen, the first point, is sometimes shortened to five. Deuce might be said at 30–30, since both players need two points to win. When recounting set scores, there is no need to mention the first number (usually six, but sometimes seven) since it is a given, so a player may say that she won in three and five, meaning 6–3, 7–5.

To prevent matches from continuing on and on when the score is 6–6, the *tiebreaker* was invented. At 6–6, the next server (the first one to begin serving that set) serves the first point to the deuce court. Then the opponent serves two points, starting from the ad court. From this point on, each player serves two points beginning in the ad court. Whenever the total score is divisible by six, the players change ends of the court but continue the service pattern. This goes on until someone reaches a minimum of seven points with a two-point margin (for example, 7–5, 7–0, 10–8).

## THE WARM-UP

Before the match starts, players warm up with each other for a period of time. At tournament-level play, only five minutes is allowed before play must begin. The tour players have warmed up extensively elsewhere and use this time as the final warm-up.

Unfortunately, many beginners do not understand the intent of the warm-up, which is to ready your shots for the play that is about to begin. Too often players inappropriately use the warm-up period to practice put-away shots or hit poorly on purpose to throw the opponent off. This leads to no warm-up for either player. Each player is obligated to warm up the opponent and should be hitting the shots back with moderate to good speed.

A player should warm up all the skills, strokes, volleys, serves, and overheads before play begins. Although many inexperienced players like to delay practicing their serve until it is their turn in the match, this is not allowed. Players should hit two or three serves, then let the opponent hit two or three. If one player continues to hit practice serves into the net instead of returning the balls across the net, the opponent will have no time to warm up the serve. This is unfair and is not allowed.

The warm-up is the place to set the tone of the match. As a player, you are out there to compete. Never try to aggravate your opponent before the match starts, or you'll be burdened with a contentious, rancorous match.

## GAME PLAY

Each player serves one game at a time, then the opponent serves. To balance out wind, sun, and other court conditions, players change sides after completing the odd games: one, three, five, and so on. In the tiebreaker, players change sides after every six points. This rule starts over with each set: For example, a set ending at 6–3 requires a side change; then after the next game—the first of the next set—players change again. If the set ends at 6–4, play continues on the same side for one more game.

Sides are changed at the end of a tiebreaker, regardless of the score. The person who served the first game of the tiebreaker set (that is, served the odd games) is now the receiver regardless of the score in the tiebreaker.

## SERVICE RULES

The *serve* begins each game. On each point, the server is given two opportunities to place the serve in the crosscourt box. The first point is always served into the left box, called the *deuce court*, and the second goes to the right service box, the *ad court*. This rotation is continued for each point. If the first serve goes into the proper square, the point is played out. If the serve is missed, the miss is called a *fault*, and the server must serve again. If this serve lands in the service box, the point is played out, but if the second serve misses, the player has *double faulted*, which results in the server's loss of that point.

If the server steps onto the baseline or crosses over the center line before making contact with the ball, the server has committed a *foot fault* and the serve is automatically deemed out. When there are no line judges, this rule is seldom enforced; however, it is one of the rules, so players should be aware of their foot placement.

If one of the serve attempts touches the net before landing in the proper service box, it is called a *let* and that serve is repeated, with no penalty. Except on the serve, whenever a hit ball touches the net and drops into the court, you must play the ball.

## CODE OF CONDUCT

To ensure the highest type of sportsmanship, the United States Tennis Association (USTA) has established a code of conduct that every player is expected to follow. The following principles and guidelines apply in any match conducted without officials:

1. If you have any doubt as to whether a ball is out or good, you must give your opponent the benefit of the doubt and play the ball as good. You should not play a let.

2. It is your obligation to call all balls on your side, to help your opponent make calls when the opponent requests it, and to *call against yourself* (with the exception of the first service) any ball that you clearly see out on your opponent's side of the net.

3. Any "out" or "let" call must be made instantaneously (i.e., before either an opponent has hit the return or the return has gone out of play); otherwise, the ball continues in play.

4. Do not enlist the aid of spectators in making line calls.

5. If you call a ball out and then realize it was good, you should correct your call.

6. To avoid controversy over the score, the server should announce the set score (e.g., 5–4) before starting a game and the game score (e.g., 30–40) before serving each point.

7. If players cannot agree on the score, they may go back to the last score on which there was agreement and resume play from that point, or they may spin a racquet.

8. Foot faults are not allowed. If an opponent persists in foot faulting after being warned not to do so, the referee should be informed.

9. Do not stall, sulk, complain, or practice gamesmanship.

10. Wait until the players on another court have completed a point before retrieving or returning a ball.

11. Once you have entered a tournament, honor your commitment to play. Exceptions should occur only in cases of serious illness, injury, or personal emergency.

12. From the beginning of the match, play must be continuous. Attempts to stall or extend rest periods for the purpose of recovering from a loss of physical condition (such as cramps or shortness of breath) are clearly illegal.

13. Intentional distractions that interfere with your opponent's concentration or effort to play the ball are against the rules.

14. Spectators, including parents, friends, and coaches, are welcome to watch and enjoy matches. Their role, however, is clearly restricted to that of passive observer with *no involvement of any kind* during the match.

15. Players are expected to put forth a full and honest effort regardless of the score or expected outcome.

16. Players are expected to maintain full control over their emotions and their behavior throughout the match. If you begin to lose your composure during play, try the following:

    a. Take several deep breaths. Exhale as slowly as possible and feel your muscles relax.

    b. Concentrate on your own game and behavior and ignore distractions from your opponent or surroundings.

    c. Be your own best friend—enjoy your good shots and forget the poor ones.

At the competitive level, there is a three-pronged penalty system for violating the rules of behavior. The first violation incurs a warning, the second costs a point, and the third results in a defaulted match. Although the pros do a certain amount of arguing with the officials, technically it is not allowed and sets a poor example.

## OTHER RULES OF THE GAME

There are a few quirky rules of the game you should know about. For example, a ball is not out until it is called out. So don't touch an out ball until it has bounced and been called out.

If the ball hits you on any part of your body before bouncing, regardless of whether you are standing inside or outside the court, the point automatically belongs to your opponent. Thus even if the ball is clearly long and you catch it on a fly, you lose the point. Even if you are diligently trying to avoid being hit but the ball nicks your foot, you have lost the point. This applies to the serve as well. In doubles, this also applies to your partner. If a clearly wide serve hits your partner on the fly, you lose the point.

You must use your racquet to hit the ball over the net. Once I was chasing a low ball and just missed it, though it did hit my foot and go over the net. Although my opponent thought that I had hit the ball with my racquet, I was obligated to inform him that it was his point. You can use any part of the racquet to hit the ball. The standard response when the ball hits the edge and goes over is, "I paid for the whole racquet, therefore I plan to use the whole racquet."

You can hit the ball only once on your side. There is a very thin line between a "carry," in which the shot is one continuous motion but the ball rolls on the racquet and gets thrown over the net like a jai alai shot, and a double hit, in which the ball has left the racquet and you contact it again before it crosses the net.

Further, you are not allowed to touch the net with your racquet or any part of your body or clothing after your shot until the ball has bounced twice. If you do, the point is over, no matter how clear it is that the ball was unreturnable.

If you touch or reach over the net or the ball hits part of your body or double bounces, you are immediately obligated to call these infractions against yourself. If you suspect that this has occurred with your opponent, continue to play the point, but at its conclusion you may ask whether the ball bounced twice or mention that a piece of clothing or body part hit the net. Because these are self-calls, the ultimate determination is the offending player's integrity.

There are a few more oddities to know about. You must let the ball cross over the net before you hit it; you must not prohibit the ball from reaching your side.

Every once in a while, due to spin or the wind, the ball will land on your side but spin or blow back over the net to the other side before you can touch it. Once the ball has landed on your side, you can reach over the net to hit the ball (the only time this is permissible), as long as you do not touch the net. Unless you have touched the ball (the only time it is permissible to reach over the net), you will lose the point, because it will be deemed that you are not responsible for its return.

If the ball you hit touches anything on or over the court, you are deemed to have missed. Thus if there are electrical wires or lights overhead and the ball hits them, you lose the point. The only thing that can be hit is the net post, which is deemed part of the court. A wide shot may be returned by going around the net, rather than over; that is legal.

In doubles, if your partner nicks the ball and you then hit it over, you lose the point. If you crash racquets but only one of the racquets hits the ball, the ball remains in play.

## SOCIAL TENNIS

When you play social tennis, there are additional unwritten rules of behavior. If all the players are equal, then everyone can play full out. When one or more players are substantially better, then the better players must tone down their game. Every Sunday morning in my singles game, I play full out; in the afternoon I play mixed doubles with my wife and various other couples. This is not my time; it is their time, so I hit the ball as if I were giving a lesson.

Some players have difficulty adjusting to social tennis; they feel that it destroys their game. However, try to think of there being three "buttons": a try button, a focus button, and a power button. Adjust only the power button in social tennis. Toning your game down does not have to mean less focus or effort.

# BASIC TENNIS ETIQUETTE

Tennis is a civilized sport that emphasizes fairness and politeness. Here are a few basic rules of etiquette:

- Leave balls on the baseline near the center mark when changing ends.
- Do not return "fault" service balls. Let them pass to the back wall.
- Do not talk when your opponent is ready to hit the ball. If a ball from another court rolls onto your court during your opponent's service motion, offer to play a let.

One final note on rules and behavior: All lines are good; if any part of the ball touches any part of the line, the ball continues to be played. The farther away you are from a ball, the more difficult it is to judge it correctly. Because of parallax, many balls landing close to the line may appear to be out, but in reality are good. Be generous with your line calls.

# TWO

## TENNIS EQUIPMENT AND CLOTHING

**A** beginning tennis player has only a few basic needs: a pair of tennis shoes and socks, tennis clothes, a racquet, and a can of tennis balls.

### SHOES

A player needs a pair of shoes made specifically for tennis; running shoes are not good substitutes. Because the heel is built up in running shoes, the sudden stops required in tennis will cause your toes to jam into the end of the shoe, which is not built for that kind of pressure. Since the toe of the shoe is not reinforced for shock and drag, you will wreck not only your toes, but the shoes as well. In addition, many running shoes have black bottoms that leave long black skid marks on the tennis court. With the cost of resurfacing a court at over $5,000, it is easy to understand why cities, clubs, and individuals become annoyed when someone wears black "skid markers" on the court.

Although aerobic and basketball shoes can be used, they were not designed for tennis. Wearing them on the tennis court substantially curtails their life because they, too, were not built to absorb the shock and drag of a tennis court. A popular new shoe, called a cross trainer, is designed to minimize the athletic footwear in your closet.

There are two main styles of tennis shoes: the familiar low-cut shoes and the new three-quarter cut. Which one is best for you is limited only by your budget and sense of comfort. The three-quarter shoe offers more ankle support but is bulkier. All the big-name companies—Nike, Reebok, New Balance, L.A. Gear, and Converse—make quality products.

Tennis shoes do not last forever; usually the toes wear out first. There are products on the market that prolong the toe or shoe life. The best is a urethane glue called Freesole (formerly called Liquid Sole).

Shoes are now available in a variety of colors. Some of the top pros recently introduced the black tennis shoe (not to be confused with the black-bottomed running shoe). This trendy black tennis shoe is a current top seller.

If your feet, ankles, or knees hurt, change shoe styles. A player can comfortably wear a particular style for over a year before developing a sudden ailment that disappears when the shoe style is changed. Even if your body does not demand a new shoe, chances are the manufacturer will, since shoe styles change almost yearly. The unwritten rule of shoe styles seems to be if you like the shoe style, it will be discontinued.

Orthotics are shoe inserts that are custom-made for your feet. They can be soft or made of plastic, and they assure a more precise, comfortable shoe fit. Most podiatrists and some sporting goods stores can make these for you. Some athletic shoe retailers have computers that customize the insert to your foot.

## APPAREL

Apparel requirements vary greatly, depending on your playing environment. In public parks, anything goes, from aerobic apparel to cutoffs. Most private clubs require the traditional tennis apparel: women in tennis dresses, skirts, or shorts; men in collared shirts and tennis shorts. T-shirts are not allowed. Although most clubs today encourage colorful attire, a few clubs still adhere to the decades-old all white dress code. Whenever playing at a club for the first time, always inquire in advance about the dress code.

Tennis clothes come in many colors and styles. Always make sure that your apparel is as comfortable as possible. When you step onto the court for a match, your clothes should not be a distraction to you.

There are three different kinds of socks: the socks that stop below the ankle, the ones that come a little above the ankle, and the traditional pull-up socks. This is personal comfort choice and fashion decision, depending on where you want your tan line. (As you increase your time on the court, your body will sport various tan lines all over.)

If you tend to perspire heavily, wristbands can keep the perspiration on your arms from rolling onto your hands. Headbands serve the same purpose, and also keep errant strands of hair out of your eyes. Often the two are sold together, in the full color spectrum, and can be coordinated with your outfit.

If the scientists are right about the depletion of the ozone layer, then most outdoor enthusiasts should don a hat or visor to protect their faces from the sun's rays. Jim Courier, 1991 French Open champion, always wears a hat, even indoors! Most clubs allow colored hats. In extreme sun, Ivan Lendl, another top player, sports a Legionnaire-type hat that protects his head, face, and neck.

## RACQUETS

Until about 28 years ago, tennis racquets came in one size and were made of wood. Since then, tennis racquet technology has exploded.

The first changes occurred in the materials. Space-age materials from graphites to metals greatly increased the power that the racquet could generate, though the size stayed the same, at 78 square inches.

The next revolution occurred in 1976. Racquet size increased to many variations between 90 and 130 square inches — the two most popular sizes being 90 and 110 square inches. At first, many players were reluctant to change over to the bigger racquets, but within five years every serious player used a larger racquet. Students were discouraged from using technologically outdated, hand-me-down racquets.

Three years ago, the technology advanced again with a new generation of racquets called *wide bodies*. Although the hitting area was not enlarged, the frame's width was, which radically transformed the power of the game. Players immediately embraced the wide-body racquets, and now all serious players use them. The power and shot-making ability of the pros have been brought to the masses through this new technology and equipment.

## Which Racquet Should You Buy?

*Children:*  For a child under six years, you should purchase a junior racquet. It is not as long as the standard 27-inch adult racquet, and the grip size is substantially smaller. Many companies make children's racquets, priced between $20 and $100.

*Beginners:*  Whether child or adult, start with a 110-sized racquet. The latest technology is not necessary, so price is the main consideration. There is a tremendous selection of good racquets priced between $40 and $100.

*Experienced and Serious Players:*  The new wide-body racquets are a must. Because every player and arm are different, a player needs the most powerful racquet the body will tolerate. The widest wide body is not necessary, but one of the wide bodies is. These more pricey racquets cost between $50 and $350.

A word to the wise about body pain: Unquestionably, the better the player's form, the less likely an injury to the back, shoulder, or elbow. Wide-body racquets are all aerodynamically light and very stiff, which can put more stress on the shoulder and elbow. If playing causes you pain in these areas, try the following adjustments:

1. Restring the racquet 10 pounds lighter.
2. Install a cushion grip.
3. Add lead tape in different locations on the racquet head to lessen the racquet's vibrations. Place tape at the 3:00 and 9:00 positions on the racquet.
4. Add a dampener, which comes in varying shapes, to the bottom string to provide additional shock absorption.

If you still have pain, trade the racquet in for a different one. No amount of shot-making ability or improvement is worth body pain or damage.

# THREE

# TECHNIQUES

## GRIPS

So, you are eager to play tennis. The first question you should ask is, How do I hold the racquet? There are many different *grips* used to hold the racquet. The key is to make a clear choice. When the ball is coming toward you, you have no time to look at your hand to make sure it has been placed correctly. The choice needs to be made and mastered. You must develop a feel or sensual awareness of the racquet's relationship to your hand.

To use the *eastern* grip on the forehand, simply shake hands with your racquet. On the backhand side, hold your index knuckle at the top of the grip. Professional players like to rotate their grip more toward the side on which they are hitting. If the rotation is slight, the grip is called *semi-western*. If the rotation is greater, it is called a *western* grip. On both sides, the more your hand is behind the racquet head, the easier it will be to square the racquet head on contact, which facilitates moving low to high on the hit, producing more topspin. However, using very different grips makes the grip change cumbersome.

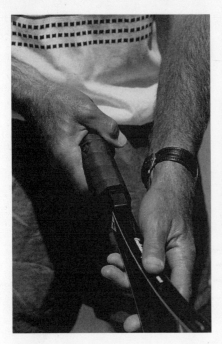

Eastern forehand

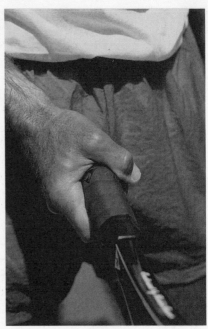

Semi-western forehand

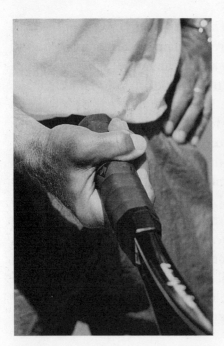

Western forehand

Continental

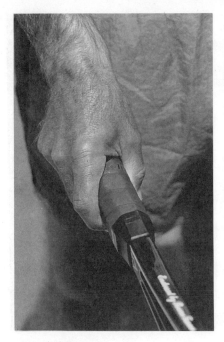

Eastern backhand

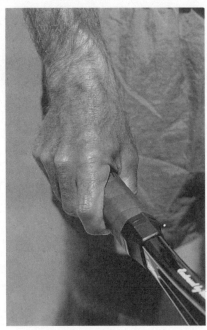

Semi-western backhand

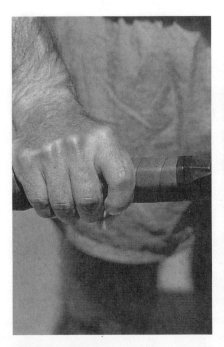

Western backhand

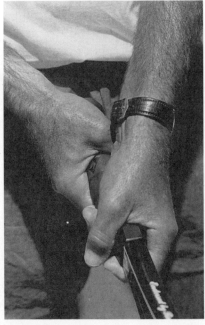

Two hands, with the right hand on the bottom

Eastern forehand

Semi-western forehand

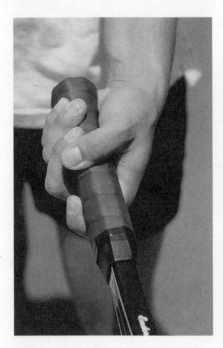

Western forehand

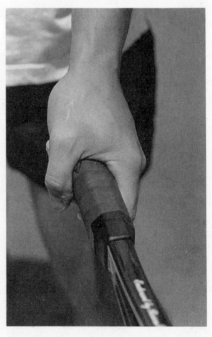

Continental

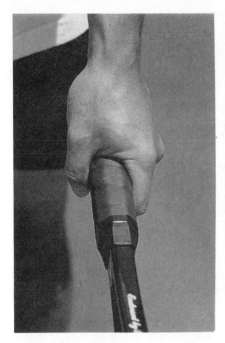

Eastern backhand

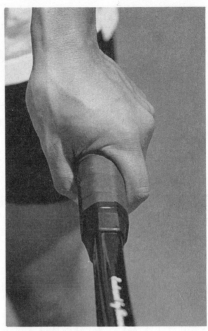

Semi-western backhand

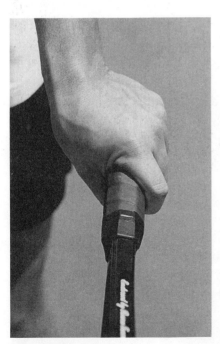

Western backhand

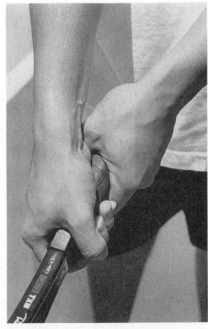

Two hands, with the left hand on the bottom

Which grip should you use? The simple answer is that it doesn't matter! Although some instructors insist that you must use a specific grip to be any good, this is simply not true. Different pros use different grips, and so can you. Grab the racquet in a way that feels comfortable. Only if you are missing badly should you experiment with the grip.

Many instructors insist that you learn to serve using the *continental* grip, which effects greater wrist action. This is true, and using a more pronounced backhand grip will further promote wrist action. But I have found that for many young players, learning to serve with this grip is too difficult. Again, just grip the racquet in a manner comfortable to you.

Instructors often insist that you learn the continental grip for volleys. Because the ball arrives sooner when you are at the net, there is less response time to hit the ball. Supposedly, maintaining one grip for both forehands and backhands maximizes the time available for stroking the ball when it arrives at your side, which should be an advantage. But you must have very strong wrist muscles to hold the one grip. The average player is better off holding the eastern forehand and eastern backhand.

Always wait in the forehand grip, and if the ball moves to your backhand side, set your racquet with the nonhitting hand, which moves the grip. As soon as the shot is completed, the nonhitting hand moves the grip back to the forehand grip. As long as the grip change is done in a two-in-one process, it doesn't take extra time.

## One Hand or Two?

Your body size and the strength in your arm and wrist determine whether to use one hand or two. There are touring players earning a million dollars using both methods. So which should you use? Again, experiment to find out which is comfortable for you. Monica Seles, the top woman player, uses two hands on both her forehand and her backhand. Some instructors insist on one or the other; ultimately, however, you are the best judge.

If you use two hands, the grip issue must still be resolved. Again, where to place your hands is up to you. Although some players like to hold a right-hand and left-hand eastern grip, others prefer to use the dominant hand in a backhand grip and the other hand in an eastern grip.

## WHERE TO STAND

Having resolved the grip and hands issues, you must know where to stand. In both singles and doubles, there are just two basic positions on the court: at the net or in the backcourt. When in the backcourt, stand two to five feet past the baseline or end line. The more aggressive your style of play, the closer you should position yourself to the baseline. At the pro level, the players who rush the net at every opportunity or step up to the ball stand closer to the baseline, and the players who are predominantly strokers stand deeper back.

When coming to the net in singles, your goal is to reach the area just short of halfway between the net and the service line, which I call the *five-eighths line*. Divide the distance between the net and service line in half, then take one small step back toward the service line, and you will be standing on the five-eighths line. When advancing toward the net, if you reach only the service line, you will be too vulnerable to angle shots and shots hit at your feet. If you move too close to the net, you will be vulnerable to lobs and shots hit with great power, because you have minimal reaction time. The five-eighth's line is the spot from which you can handle all the possibilities your opponent may throw at you.

When you serve in singles, stand within two side steps of the middle of the tennis court so you can cover the entire court. It's not a good idea to stand way outside on the backhand court, even though some pros do. Andre Agassi, 1992 Wimbledon champion, likes to stand as far left as possible on occasion, so that he can bounce his serve very wide to his opponent's backhand, which forces the opponent to hit to Agassi's forehand, his strength. For a baseline player, this is occasionally a good strategy.

The baseline position

The five-eighths line

The deuce court position for singles

The ad court position for singles

The deuce court position for doubles

The ad court position for doubles

When you serve in doubles, again stand within two steps of the middle of your responsibility zone. The best place is halfway between the middle of the court and the doubles out-of-bounds line.

When you return service in singles, stand inside the singles line about six inches; this bisects the angle that the server can hit. Again, if you are trying to protect a side because you have no confidence in your forehand or backhand, or your opponent serves to only one location, you can make adjustments. In doubles, the positioning is similar.

In doubles, each player is responsible for one-half of the court —not the front or back half, but the left or right half. The server should be positioned nearly in the middle of the area covered. The server's partner should stand in the middle of the service box at the five-eighths line. Too many young players stand in the alley, and others camp out too close to the net.

Again, the serve returner must bisect the server's angle. As the server in doubles hits wider, so must the returner flow wider to cover the new angle possibilities. The returner's partner traditionally

Serve return. The position on the deuce court

Serve return. The position on the ad court

stands on the service line or back a few feet for defensive purposes, in case the returner hits a poor return, and to help call the service line. At the pro level, this person starts at the five-eighths line, which is a more aggressive position. There is an assumption that the return will be aggressive, so the net person wants to be positioned closer to the net to take full advantage.

If you have no confidence or ability at the net, it is permissible to have both players start in the backcourt. At the pro level, you will see some teams returning serve with both players back at the baseline. This occurs when the serving side is so dominant that the returning side is having difficulty returning the serve or avoiding the net person.

In serving to the deuce court:

A. The server is halfway between the middle and the doubles out-of-bounds line.

B. The server's partner is standing at the five-eighths line in the middle of the service square.

C. The serve returner is back by the baseline on the deuce court.

D. The returner's partner is on the service line. The second picture shows her on the five-eighths line.

In serving to the ad court:

A. The server is halfway between the middle of the court and the doubles out-of-bounds line.

B. The server's partner is standing at the five-eighths line in the middle of the service square.

C. The returner.

D. The returner's partner is on the service line. The second picture shows him at the five-eighths line.

# HOW TO MOVE

Tennis is a sport in which you must use three spatial extenders: your leg, your arm, and your racquet. Most people don't think about moving their feet; it just happens. When James Brady, President Reagan's press secretary, was recovering from head wounds, he commented that he had to watch his steps because he had lost the awareness of his leg positioning. When people start to play tennis, they too lose awareness of their leg positioning.

There is a specific look that you need to achieve as you try to catch up to the ball on the tennis court. Your initial position on the court is called the *ready position*; this is how you stand when you are ready to receive the hit ball. Your shoulders are parallel to the net, your knees are slightly bent, and your body weight is distributed so that the upper body is on top of the lower body. The footwork pattern is the same for both right- and left-handers.

The body balanced for the ready position

When a ground stroke comes to your right side, you must rotate your shoulders to that side and step in with the left leg. When the ground stroke comes to your left side, rotate your shoulders to the left and step in on your right foot. That sounds simple enough, but the key is the leg with which you step in. On each shot you must make a spatial adjustment for this leg. You may have to step away from the ball or more closely into the path of the ball. Some pros do not step at all, preferring to use an *open stance*, which helps them prepare for the next shot more quickly.

## PHILOSOPHY OF MOVEMENT

Now that you know where to stand and how to move, you need to learn the philosophy of movement. The first rule is that you must play as if every ball you hit will land inside the court. Because of that mind-set, you must reposition to one of the two basic locations discussed earlier. Unfortunately, too many inexperienced players use the time it takes the ball to travel to the opponent's side as a dead rest period, which creates many problems. When you act like a light switch, turning on and off, it becomes too difficult to turn back on again because you are often unaware that you have turned off. By standing still as the ball travels to the other side, you leave a large part of the court unattended, which tells your opponent where to hit the next shot. Further, you greatly increase your opponent's incentive for chasing the ball, because it is obvious you have quit the point. Your opponent knows that if he can just hit the ball back over the net, he will win the point.

The second rule of movement is to play as if every ball your opponent hits will land inside the court. Therefore, you must react to and chase every ball. Don't make a judgment about whether the ball will land in or out; move to the ball as soon as it has been struck. Is it going short or deep? Left or right? Inexperienced players wait for the ball to approach rather than moving off the hit. Tennis is supposed to be a sport of exercise, so move to burn some calories.

As your opponent hits the ball to a specific location, you must win the race to that spot. If you arrive there before the ball, you will

The shoulders turn to the right

A more open stance to get away from the ball

A parallel step into the court

A further crossover to reach out more

The shoulders turn to the left

More open

Parallel

More closed

have plenty of time to prepare for your shot. To use a basketball analogy: you must deny the ball the court position; get to the spot first. Once there, secure that spot so that you can hit the shot on balance. If you watch the ball and keep your head and body quiet, you will easily execute the shot. If you are off balance and your head is moving about, your odds of success are greatly diminished.

## THE SHOTS

There are three categories of shots in tennis: ground strokes, meaning the ball has bounced once; balls hit on the fly, before they bounce; and the serve. In each of the shot sections I illustrate one basic technique, then explain a few variations. For all the shots, it is imperative that you answer the following five questions:

1. How will you grip the racquet — including how many hands will you use?
2. How do you want to start the shot?
3. How do you want to hit the shot? With underspin? Topspin? Flat?
4. What rhythm will you use on the speed of hit?
5. How will you follow through?

The key to tennis success is to tailor a form that is right for you. One of the top golf coaches once said that there is no one standard golf swing for everyone, but there is a golf swing for everyone. The same is true for tennis. As you watch 12 different tennis pros play, you may see 12 variations. Although there will be some similarities and some differences, each player will have a distinctive shot. In my explanations of the shots, I give you the most basic choices; however, they may not be productive for you, so you must make each shot your own by using the five-question guideline.

When you first begin to play tennis, all the hits feel the same. Nothing feels right and nothing feels wrong, because you have no sensual awareness of your body movement, and you are easily confused. You may hit four shots, all of which feel the same, even though two may land in, one in the net, and one long. Because the shots all felt the same, you may unfortunately conclude that since the form doesn't always work, you must "reinvent" the shot on any given day. Once you understand that the form never fails you, though you may fail the form, correction is easy—just review the five questions.

Tony Gwynn of the San Diego Padres is one of the best hitters in major league baseball today. He believes that there are three key factors in his hitting success, and they can be adapted to hitting a tennis ball. First, Gwynn likes to keep his hands nice and loose on the bat—the soft hands theory. Soft hands help your body relax; when you grip too tightly, your entire body freezes up. Beginning tennis players often try to grip the racquet more tightly when they feel it turn in their hands. But the racquet torques because the ball was hit on the perimeter of the racquet rather than in the center. So if your racquet moves, track the ball better instead of gripping more tightly.

Second, Gwynn believes that in baseball the goal is not to hit the ball but to follow through, watching the ball and hitting along the swing path. This is true in tennis as well as the other hitting sports. Many players stop the shot motion when making contact with the ball. As a result, the ball doesn't have enough propulsion to go over the net.

His third point is to follow through to the same finish spot each time. In tennis this is critical. If you change your follow-through every time, you will never master your shots. The goal is to hit through the ball, not stopping your swing until you reach your mastered follow-through spot.

## Forehand Ground Stroke

There are three kinds of ground strokes: flat, topspin, and underspin. The basic shot described here is a moderate topspin shot. If you lower the incline of the follow-through you will hit a flatter ball.

To achieve an underspin on the hit, instead of moving low to high on the ball, move high to low, ensuring that the racquet's bottom edge is slightly ahead of the rest of the racquet, then drive through the shot.

*Footwork:* Right-handers turn right, left-handers turn left, step forward toward the net with the opposite leg.

### The Stroke:

1. The basic grip: eastern forehand. Shake hands, grabbing the racquet. Usually you use just one hand, but children or weak adults may wish to use two.
2. To start: with the racquet in front of your body pointing at the net, bring the racquet straight back, waist level, toward the back wall.
3. To hit: square up the racquet in front of you.
4. The rhythm: 75% power.
5. To finish: move the racquet slowly, inclining upward so that the shoulder of your hitting arm touches your chin, the elbow reaches your eye level. Your wrist should be at your head and the racquet head slightly above your head, thus a "ski slope" upward.

The ready position

Turn the right shoulder, and bring the racquet back at waist level

Hit with the racquet squared up in front

Follow through so that the shoulder touches or kisses the chin

In each of the above steps, you may vary the response to better fit your game, except on the rhythm issue, which should remain at 75%.

*Options:* The *slice forehand* is executed in much the same manner. At waist level, open up the racquet face with a slight high-to- low contact point on the ball. Drive up on the ball rather than chopping down at it.

The *whip and roll shot*, similar to the one used by Boris Becker, the youngest male player ever to win Wimbledon, starts with a loop. Although the contact point is still flat in front of you, you whip and roll the racquet on contact so that the finish is a quarter-circle turn upside down. Many people like to finish over their shoulder to ensure greater success. Do *not* finish with your racquet head down below your waist; finish high. The position checklist includes the elbow at chin level and the hand around or over the opposite shoulder.

You may also wish to *dip* start.

To slice hit, the racquet's bottom edge leads

The loop start

The roll finish

The dip start

Advanced players sometimes use an *in-out forehand*, similar to the slice. At the end, you dip the head down a little bit, then turn it outward to produce an out slice on the ball.

41

## Backhand Ground Stroke

*Footwork:* Right-handers turn to the left, left-handers turn to the right, then step forward with the opposite leg.

*The Stroke:*

1. The basic grip: eastern backhand, one-handed.
2. To start: carry the racquet straight back at waist level, with the racquet pointing to the back wall.
3. To hit: the racquet face should be squared up in front of the body.
4. The rhythm: 75% power.
5. To finish: swing the racquet on a graduated incline so that the shoulder reaches the chin, the elbow the eyes. The wrist reaches to the head, and the racquet head is above the head.

For two-handed hitters, the dominant hand grips in an eastern backhand and the other hand in an eastern forehand. Alternatively, both

The ready position

Turn the shoulders to the right side

Hit with the racquet face squared up      Follow through shoulder to chin

hands can be positioned in an eastern forehand grip. To start, pull the racquet straight back at waist level to the back wall. On the hit, square up in front, using 75% rhythm. To finish, the nondominant arm becomes the check arm — shoulder to chin, elbow to eyes, wrist to head, racquet over the head in a ski slope incline.

There is a third choice that some pros use, combining the best of both — hitting with two hands, but finishing with one hand. Again, the pros use all three styles to earn millions. Play with the options to see which works best for you.

*Options:* The *slice* backhand starts at the waist. Come across the ball, a little high to low on the ball, not chopping down, but extending upward. On the in-to-out shot, slice and turn out the racquet head. The *Becker backhand*, also known as the *roll shot*, begins like the left-handed forehand. Whip it over and roll it, trying to get the racquet over the shoulders. On the backhand start you can also loop up or dip the start or kick the racquet up. All three generate more head speed because of the increased swing path.

The two-handed grip

Turn the shoulders to the left side

Hit with the racquet face squared in front

Finish left shoulder kissing the chin, racquet head over head level stretched straight out

The two-handed let-go-at-the-end finish

The slice one-handed shot, with the bottom edge leading

The in-to-out finish; the edge of the racquet leads slightly

The two-handed whip and roll finish

A loop start on the backhand

A dip start on the backhand

A kick start

## Forehand Volleys

*Footwork:* With your toes pointing toward the net, step in with the opposite leg on the hit side. A right-hander would step with the left leg, a left-hander with the right leg.

*The Stroke:*

1. The basic grip: eastern forehand or continental.
2. To start: place hands in front, turned to the forehand side at a 90-degree angle.
3. The hit: lead slightly with the bottom edge or square-up the racquet face.
4. The rhythm: 75%.

The ready position

Racquet head to the right, shoulders squared to the net

**49**

The punch follow-through          The quarter-circle finish

**5.** To finish: for the *punch method*, punch out in front of the body, leaving the racquet head at a 90-degree angle; for the *quarter-circle method*, follow through so the racquet head is facing the opponent's back wall.

## Backhand Volley

*Footwork:* Point your toes toward net. Step in with the leg opposite the hit side. Right-handers step with the right leg, left-handers with the left leg.

*The Stroke:*

1. The grip: eastern backhand or continental.
2. To start: place your hands to the backhand side.

The ready position

Racquet head to the left, shoulders square to the net

**3.** To hit: slightly lead with the bottom edge of the racquet or square-up the racquet head.

**4.** The rhythm: 75%.

**5.** To finish: for the punch method, punch forward so the tip of the racquet is still at a 90-degree angle; for the quarter-circle method, the follow-through brings the racquet head around to face the opponent's back wall.

Most pros do not use two hands on the backhand volley; however, for strength or comfort you may wish to do so. On strokes and volleys you may wonder what the difference is between using one hand versus two. There really isn't much difference. When you use two hands, you lose about three inches of range on the wide shots. If your opponent hits the ball that well, you are going to lose anyway,

The punch follow-through

The quarter-circle follow-through

A two-handed start of the racquet

The two-handed punch

The two-handed quarter-circle finish

so how many hands you use on the racquet is inconsequential. But the other 80% of the balls that your opponent hits you must handle. He will hit some you can't reach, and you will hit some he cannot reach, which is an equalizer. Therefore, you must design your shots for the eight in ten you must reach. Again, strength and personal comfort should be the two determining factors in your decision.

## Half Volley

A *half volley* is a shot hit like a volley at the net, but the ball bounces before contact is made. When you are at the net you should try to hit everything on the fly. If the ball is low, bend down to the plane of the ball. If it lands first you will already be low. Use your volley form and hit up on the ball.

The forehand half volley

The backhand half volley

## The Serve

*The Toss:* Both arms are important during the service motion. One arm tosses the ball into the right location so the racquet arm can hit the ball. But *toss* is actually a misnomer, since it implies that you must *throw* the ball. Executed with your nondominant arm, which many people rarely use, the motion is not a toss but a swing of the arm's momentum that will carry the ball into the air every time.

There are five parts to the toss:

1. Use the same downswing spot on your leg: Drop your toss hand downward to the front of your thigh, making sure that the back of your hand stops at the same location on every toss attempt.

2. Use the same upswing spot every time. Always place your hand in the same spot. As you swing your arm, your elbow, wrist, and hand should face toward you at all times.

3. Use the same rhythm to swing your arm every time.

4. Use the same release door — only the top door, not the side door — every time.

Starting the toss at the downswing spot

The upswing spot and the release

The toss arm collapses onto the body; the left hand
falls into the right shoulder

**5.** When your tossing arm comes down, let it collapse softly into
your body. Some pros hold the toss arm up longer than others.
What matters is the collapsing action. Most beginners whip their
arms and then lose their balance and the ability to keep their
heads up.

*Toss Location:*   In describing the toss location, we use a clock. The
toss location range is from 11:00 to 1:00. The primary location is
toward your hitting side. Thus for a player who is right-handed, the
toss goes to the 1:00 location. A lefty's toss location is 11:00. All
tosses should be one and a half to three feet in front of you. By
changing the toss location ever so slightly, you can change the spin
of the serve.

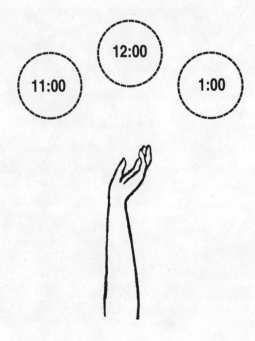

For the pros, I developed a five-serve theory of toss location. For all five serves, tosses are placed out in front of the body, at least one and a half to three feet into the court. The *second serve* is tossed at 11:00. The *hard kick serve*, particularly effective wide to the backhand side, is placed at 11:59. The *hard topspin*, a good base serve, is tossed at 12:00. A *heated serve*, at 12:01, is a hard slider or flat serve. The *slice*, particularly effective wide to the forehand and into the body, is placed at 12:03.

***Toss Height:*** There is some debate on how high the toss height should be. Different pros use different techniques. The most powerful servers in the game toss low and try to make contact with the ball at the height of the toss. Roscoe Tanner, who has the fastest recorded serve, did this but it is very difficult to gauge the time, so very few other pros do it. Most pros toss the ball slightly higher than they can reach and let the ball fall into the hit zone.

*Footwork:*  The traditional alignment pattern requires facing sideways and placing your feet so that if you drew a line from your back foot through the front foot, it would go into the service square that you are targeting. Advanced positioning allows for showing more of your back. On the forehand service box side, your back foot is aligned with the heel of your right foot. On the backhand side, your back foot is turned more toward the back wall. John McEnroe does this in the extreme by placing both feet on the service line; all the top players use a modified version of this positioning, which I call the *baby McEnroe* stance.

The traditional deuce court footwork

The baby McEnroe stance for the deuce court

The traditional ad court footwork

The baby McEnroe stance for the ad court

## The Service Hit:

1. The basic grip: eastern forehand. More advanced players use the continental; very advanced, the full backhand.

2. To start: from your waist, let the racquet drop down and begin to make a counterclockwise circle.

3. To hit: when the racquet reaches shoulder height, let it collapse down your back. From this position, throw your racquet up and out at the ball, hitting the ball on its bottom side.

4. The rhythm: 75% to 100%.

5. To finish: after contact, continue to swing, letting the racquet fall down across your body, producing a hugging effect.

The serve start

The racquet drop

The stretch back to the height of the shoulder

The racquet dropping down the back

The hitting motion — throwing the racquet up and out

The finish in the double hugging position; the left hand is headed toward the right shoulder, and the hitting arm is hugging the left hip

In addition to the arm-release technique, you must also coordinate a body-weight transfer with the toss. To place the toss in front of your body, it is important that you release the toss when your weight moves forward. If you toss with your weight going backward or staying neutral, it is very difficult to place the toss in front of your body.

When serving, your weight transfers from your front foot to your back foot to your front foot, in a one, two *and* three rhythm. The toss occurs on the *and* part, after the two beat. On the two beat, your arm swings down; on the *and* beat, your arm swings up before releasing the ball. A second choice would be to start with your weight on the back foot, then swing forward.

The weight transfer on the front foot        Weight transferred to the back foot

Weight transferred back to the front foot

Starting with the weight on the back foot

Leaning forward to the front foot

All big-time servers add a double knee bend to their serve that occurs when the racquet drops down the back; knees and racquet go down together, and knees and racquet go up together. There are two choices: some pros, like Boris Becker and Pete Sampras, keep their feet apart, called a *platform stance*. Others, like Stephan Edberg, bring their feet together, called a *pinpoint stance*.

There are three ways the service hit can go into the service square. You can hit down on the ball and angle it in; hit up on the ball, imparting spin; or bunt the ball and pray that it dies in time to land in the box.

Films of the service motion show that you must hit the ball from a height of 10 feet in order to be able to hit down and have the ball clear the net. Until I hurt my shoulder over 10 years ago, I thought that's what I did. Because there is too little margin for error, no pro does this anymore, even the ones who are 6'8". Everyone

The knee bend with the feet apart        The knee bend with the feet together

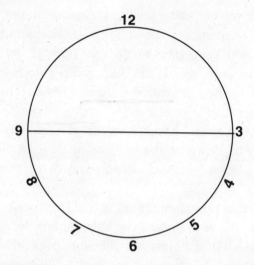

hits *up*. Thus there is a second clock: the hit on the ball clock. To hit up, the right-handed player hits from 4:00 to 7:00 on the ball; the lefty from 5:00 to 8:00. If you divide the ball into a top side and a bottom side, the top resembles a frown, the bottom a smile; always hit the smile.

Placement of the serve in the service box is an important factor. In the Move-the-Ball-Theory of serving, you maintain the same speed, but work the corners of the service square. Especially for the player who serves and volleys, maintaining a high speed serve is critical.

## Second Serve

What the advanced player tries to do on the second serve is move the toss more to the left (for a right-handed player), which forces more arching of the back and bending of the knees. This arching and bending causes the player to get under the ball more, which gives more topspin or low-to-high contact to the hit.

A second choice would be to toss the ball more to the right (for a right-handed player) and cut the ball, imparting slice. Another option is to follow the first-serve motion but use less power and speed.

If the serve is proving too tough to master because of the many increments, try starting the hit arm in the drop-down position, the way Jay Berger, a former top-20-ranked player, did.

The short start motion for second serves.

## Service Return

The *service return* is similar to a ground stroke. After the serve is hit toward you, you must hit the ball after its first bounce. You use the same footwork, racquet grips, and movement as with the ground stroke. However, there is a specific five-point form to use:

**1.** Start with one foot back on the red or behind the baseline;

**2.** Step up into the court area;

**3.** Split step;

**4.** Step in; and

**5.** Drive your arm(s) forward.

If your opponent is blasting the ball past you on serves, try treating the power serve more like a volley and block it back.

The ready position

Take one step forward

Do a balance split step

Read the serve and turn your shoulders

Drive the finish through

## Lob

The *lob* is a shot you hit high into the air to make it go over the net player's head. It is hit like a ground stroke, but on the defensive lob, you open the racquet face on the hit and incline it more upward on the follow-through. For the offensive lob, square up the racquet face on the hit, then incline the face upward.

The offensive lob requires you to be on balance so you will have many hit options; try to hit a high clearance shot over the net player's head. Hit the defensive lob when you are in trouble — usually when you are off balance, scrambling to retreat for the opponent's shot. On this shot try more height, hoping to push your opponent back off the net, ensuring yourself more time to recover and stabilize the point.

The hit for the defensive forehand lob    The finish for the defensive lob

The start for the offensive lob; get in the low-to-high position
with the racquet

The finish for the offensive lob

The hit for the defensive backhand lob

The finish for the defensive lob

The start for the offensive lob; the racquet head dips

The finish for the offensive lob

## Overhead

An *overhead* is the counter to the lob. The player tries to smash the ball, making contact much higher in the air.

*Footwork:* Similar to the service motion, turn sideways, moving your feet behind the perceived hit point, stepping back up into the ball.

*The Stroke:*

1. The basic grip: same as the service grip.
2. To start: move your hands up instantly toward the racquet drop-down position.
3. To hit: hit the ball like the serve, spinning it up to a corner.
4. The rhythm: 75%.
5. The finish: like the serve, hit through the ball and follow through, hugging your side opposite the hit.

Get the racquet up quickly

Drop the racquet down your back

Throws the racquet up and out at the ball

Follow through like the serve, across the body in the hug spot

## Dip Shot:

Usually used on passing shots, a *dip shot* is hit by coming up on the ball very quickly. By leaving the contact point early, the shot has no depth. Pros love this shot, referring to it as a two-shot pass. The goal is to dip it over and make your opponent hit up; then you'll have an easier pass.

The forehand dip shot finish

The backhand dip shot finish

## Drop Shot

By heavily slicing and just nicking the ball, you can make it die. Some like to chop the finish. The *drop shot* can also be hit by shortening the stroke and bunting the ball. For the *drop volley*, pull the racquet back on contact. A gentle touch will dampen the shot.

The forehand hit                    The forehand nick finish

The forehand chop finish

The backhand hit

The backhand nick finish

The backhand chop finish

Drop volley: The forehand hit

The pull-back dampening

The backhand hit

The pull-back dampening

## Angle Volley

To hit a *wide angle volley*, a must response to dip passes, start your racquet at a 60-degree angle instead of 90 or 110 degrees for in to out.

As I have already stated, the form never fails you, but you can fail the form. On each of the shots you learn, you need the words to describe the shot, a sensual awareness of how the shot feels, and a visual of the shot — a video — in your head. When you miss a shot, Jim Loehr, a renowned sports psychologist, recommends that you take a practice swing, executing the shot as it should be done with your eyes closed. To further reinforce the correct motion, I say rerun your video.

 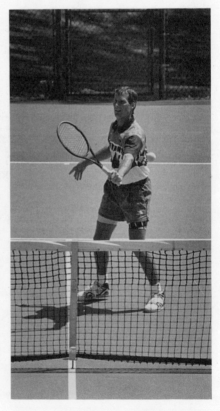

The forehand wide-out angle volley     The backhand wide-out angle volley

The in-to-out angle forehand

The in-to-out angle backhand

# FOUR

# COMMON MISTAKES AND THEIR CURES

**W**hy do you miss shots? One mistake can generate a series of domino mistakes. Often the first mistake is incorrect court positioning, which causes panic and an unorthodox shot. Once you learn the proper stroke mechanics, the single most important skill is visual perception. There is an old baseball adage that says that the fielding team must move off the crack of the bat. It is the same in tennis. As your opponent strikes the ball, four things are irrevocably determined:

1. Whether the ball is moving to your left or right;
2. Whether the ball will land short or deep;
3. At what speed the ball is moving; and
4. What kind of spin is on the ball.

Your ability to take a picture of your opponent's hit, see how the ball enters and exits the racquet, and then analyze the picture before sending the information to your feet determines your success in tennis. Unfortunately, most novice players are so focused on their side of the net, on themselves, that there is no room in their computers to analyze the other side, which creates a catch-22. If you have great form but cannot judge where the ball will land, you will be unable to hit it.

## HOW TO READ A SHOT

What are you looking for when you try to read your opponent's shot? You want to see the ball enter and exit the racquet, notice whether the ball is moving to the left or the right, look at the drive direction and the angle of the hit. Sometimes your opponent's body direction will tip the direction of the ball.

What makes a shot go deep? First, look at the clearance height over the net. The higher the clearance height, the deeper the ball will travel. Next notice if the ball was struck early and in front of the opponent, thus maximizing the body drive. Look and listen to see if the ball was struck in the middle of the racquet. A solid hit maximizes the racquet's power. Did the opponent drive through the ball? A good drive increases the depth.

What makes a ball fall short? Again, check the clearance. Very few players have the power to drive the ball deep with a low clearance shot. Recognize that a low clearance shot means that the ball will land short. There are six other reasons a ball will land short:

1. Your opponent isn't hitting the ball firmly, with good follow-through.

2. Your opponent executes a drop shot by babying the ball on purpose.

3. Your shot jammed the opponent so much that her body blocks her swing.

**4.** The ball is abandoned early because either your opponent swung up quickly or his wrist caved in.

**5.** Your opponent is late making contact with your shot and is unable to use his full body movement.

**6.** The ball is struck off-center, minimizing the racquet's power.

## Anticipation

Anticipation requires understanding the possibilities and the odds. For example, if your ball is struck deep to a corner, the opponent's return can only flow through certain geometric flight areas to remain inside the court. Thus, you flow and hedge to those areas. When you hit a hard, deep shot, the odds of a weak return increase, so look for a weak return. By watching your opponent's body, you will be able to tell where the next ball will be hit.

During the match you must search for any repeat tendencies your opponent has. Some players execute the same shots to the same areas over and over. As long as they continue to win doing that, why should they stop? If you can recognize those tendencies and counter them, you will neutralize your opponent's plan. For example, if Ms. A on the backhand court serves four straight balls short and wide to your backhand, stop looking for the forehand serve and hedge over to where the ball has been going.

## Guessing

There is a time when you want to guess on the court. For example, when your shot is so weak that your opponent clearly has the advantage and an apparent winning shot, you simply guess what his action will be and try to steal back the point. If your opponent is at the net and you hit a very weak set-up shot, guess and run to one of the corners. The very act of your moving may distract your opponent, or you may guess right and steal back the point.

# HOW TO TRACK THE BALL

There are two judgment skills involved in ground strokes and volleys: *Eye-hand coordination* enables you to recognize that the ball is going to cross your body at a certain place, and *spatial judgment* involves the leg, arm, and racquet as spatial extenders (previously discussed in Chapter 3).

## Seeing the Ball

There is some controversy over whether you can actually see the ball hit your racquet. Twelve years ago, when I invented my pre-tennis program for children, I read a study of baseball hitters. Of the 48 players studied, only two — one being Ted Williams, one of the greatest hitters ever — could actually see the ball hit the bat. One of the top gurus of tennis hypothesizes that most players lose the ball in the last six feet of the approach to the hit. People who can't see six feet in front of themselves are legally blind. I have had more success telling players to keep their heads quiet during the hit than constantly reminding them to watch the ball.

One further point on watching the ball better: Try to bring your eyes close to or on the path of the incoming ball. It is much easier to sight when you are looking on the same plane than when you are looking down two feet above the line of the ball.

## Spatially Extending Your Arm

Your arm should swing close to your body. On the swing and throughout the contact time with the ball, your elbows should stay close to your body before extending. If your arm is pinned against your body, you will have no swing. If your arm is too far away from your body, you will not be using your entire body and will be too disjointed.

## Finding the Sweet Spot

Although the standard size racquet is 27 inches long, the optimum contact point, called the *sweet spot*, is quite small. Hitting the ball with the sweet spot increases the degree of power and control. Because it is impossible to look at your racquet and the ball at the same time, it is important to develop a standard swing so you become sensually aware of your racquet's movement.

If you continually miss the center of the racquet when contacting the ball, watch the ball longer and keep your head and body still on contact. When you throw your body out of control, it is difficult to keep your head still. And if your head pulls up before or during the hit, your alignment will be off.

What if you are executing properly but still miss? Try a larger racquet size. The larger the hitting area, the greater the chance of success. Try choking up on the racquet; move your hands closer to the throat of the racquet. The less the distance between your hand and the strings, the easier it is to connect with the ball. If you are still having trouble, eliminate the leg extension and just use the arm and racquet, called hitting with an *open stance*. The economy of motion using only two spatial extenders may improve your success.

## WHERE AND WHEN TO STRIKE THE BALL

The easiest place to strike the ball is on its down flight, a little below your waist. Unfortunately, your opponent does not always hit the ball in the perfect location for you to execute your shot at that position.

There are two theories on hitting the ground strokes. One theory contends that you should try to hit every ball at the perfect height, and there are two ways of doing this. First, you can run all over like a maniac to put yourself in position to hit the ball when it drops down to the perfect height. The problem with this action is that you will often run out of court space on deep shots. Second, you can defend your territory and jump to reach the same hit height, which many pros do. This requires great timing and jumping ability.

The second theory contends that you should play the ball as it lays. With few exceptions, you defend a territory by either rising up or sinking down, like an elevator. The timing is difficult; you must

A jumping forehand

beat the ball to the plane on which it is traveling and be there to greet it. You use your knees to move your entire body up or down to meet and greet the ball. For volleys, there is only one theory of hitting height, The Play-it-as-it-Lays theory—you must deal with the ball at the height at which it comes to you.

To get to the low balls, you must bring your body down together as a unit. Your legs must be strong enough to support your weight in this position for a second or two. Most people are either right-footed or left-footed, and it is common to favor one side over the other. Your goal is to master the footwork for both sides.

A low forehand knee bend

A high forehand knees up

A low backhand knee hend

A high backhand knees up

Many new players bend only at the waist, as if to touch their toes, which throws the upper body way ahead of the lower body, forcing the weight and head down. Not only are you badly off balance, but watching the ball becomes increasingly difficult. Others lazily drop the racquet instead of bending the knees. This creates an up angle and leads to a floating shot, which, if you are lucky, may die in time to land in the court. Usually, the ball will go long; the few that do go in set up your opponent.

The rest of the chapter addresses specific problems and how to correct them.

## GROUND STROKE CORRECTIONS

*If You're Hitting into the Net:* You are making contact too late and failing to generate enough body power. Prepare earlier. Your wrist may be rolling over or caving in. Hit the ball dead center so the impact of the hit doesn't turn your racquet so forcefully. You may have missed the ball: Watch the ball better, keep your head down and still longer. If the stroke feels good and looks good but still lands in the net, then your alignment was over the ball, without enough low-to-high hit. To correct, bend down more.

If the stroke feels awful and the ball went nowhere, your body moved but your arm and racquet did not. Make sure you act and move as a team unit: upper body, lower body, arm, and racquet all moving together at the same time.

*If You're Hitting the Ball Wide:* Your balance may be pulled too much toward the aimed direction; balance better. Or you may have aimed too wide. Don't go for the lines; rather, aim in a target area with a greater margin of error.

*If You're Hitting the Ball Long:* You may be hitting slightly late. When there is not enough spin placed on the hit, it misses some gravitational resistance. To correct, attack the ball; don't let the ball play you. If the ball floats long, your racquet head probably dropped below the wrist, so remember to keep the racquet head up. This is straight geometry: If your racquet creates an up angle, the ball will go up.

If you powered the ball long, either you slapped at the ball with your wrist (an excellent hockey form, but a lousy tennis form) or your arm and racquet exploded. To correct slapping, swing your arm and racquet together as a unit. To correct exploding, remind yourself that tennis is a boundary sport and learn to harness your energy. If your arm and racquet win the race with the rest of your body, the shot will sail. Remember the team-unit movement concept.

## VOLLEY CORRECTIONS

*If You're Missing into the Net or Long:* You may be taking too much of a backswing, which is the most common volley mistake. Too much backswing results in a late and wild hit, which sends the ball all over the court. To correct, make sure that your racquet starts in front of you. Try to keep the racquet head within your sight; if the racquet is behind you, this will be impossible. The second biggest mistake is running through the volley. It is critical that when your opponent hits the ball you do a split step or neutral step that puts your body on balance, so you will be able to move in the direction of the incoming ball.

If you are missing into the net because you are mis-hitting, track the ball better. Don't look where the ball is going to go. Don't peek at the destination. Your wrist caves in, so the ball goes nowhere. Brace better for the impact.

*If Your Volleys Are Wide:* Don't go for so much precision. Also, make sure that your racquet is not angled so severely that it is impossible for the ball to land in the court.

*If Your Volleys Are Long:* Don't slap your wrist. Make sure that your racquet head stays above your wrist. If the racquet drops, the racquet angle makes the ball go up.

## SERVICE MOTION CORRECTIONS

*If Your Service Toss Is All Over the Map:* You are not giving yourself a chance of success. This is where new players often get stuck. If every toss varies greatly, so will every hit motion in reaction to the varied toss. Since every toss is an adventure in space, there is no growth pattern. To correct, slow down; make sure the tossing arm is relaxed. Then work on the five elements of the toss. Remember to make sure your toss is released as you go forward.

To help target your toss, toss the ball into a basketball hoop or into a post at the side of the court. For some players, the toss clock is too vague. By using a real target, they can better visualize the toss-control concept.

*If Your Service Hit Misses into the Net:* You have hit down on the ball, giving the geometric angle no chance of clearing the net. If your toss was not high enough in the first place, reaching only as

Practice tosses into the pole

Practice tosses into the basket

high as your nose, you will find it difficult to hit up. Swing the toss-ing arm more to get more toss height. Your tossing hand and your head may have come down too soon. Many players are so worried about hitting the tossing arm that they yank it away quickly, which pulls their shoulders and weight down. Or you may have looked too soon to see where the hit ball will land, which also pulls the head down too soon, with the rest of the body following. Keep your toss-ing arm and head up longer. Try to sight the toss through your toss-ing hand, which forces you to stay tall on the serve.

If your toss was good initially but was too low by the time you hit the ball, you didn't go up to the ball. This is a tough one for be-ginning players. What allows you to serve the ball with a constant speed is the belief that the toss is going to be in the same approxi-mate location every time. If the toss is always radically different, it is nearly impossible to spot and find the errant toss. To correct, trust your toss and stay aggressive. If you serve in segments the power goes away; go up after the ball.

Did you did bend your knees enough? For those of you who have added the knee bend, this is a big part of your motion and helps you get under the ball. Learn to relax and not rush your mo-tion. You must incorporate this integral part each time.

*If Your Service Motion Is Long:* The toss is behind you. You are hit-ting the ball too early in the motion. Try tossing the ball more in front of you. Did you push it long? If the toss is too low, you will get under it and just push it up. Try tossing the ball higher. Your feet may have moved too much. If you move your feet you get no wrist action, because the toss will be either too far right or left. You will come out of the over-your-head motion and push the ball out. Bring the toss back into the target range.

*If Your Service Motion is Wide:* Remember that when you serve you must drive your motion into the target box. Don't aim too finely; don't go for the lines. Give yourself a wider target area. New players especially should aim for the middle of the square on the second serve to prevent double faulting.

## OVERHEAD CORRECTIONS

*If Your Overhead Lands in the Net:* The ball dropped too low. When the ball drops too low, it is difficult not to overhit it down, resulting in no clearance. To correct, prepare earlier and reach up more. If you are mis-hitting — hitting the edge of your racquet — the ball will go nowhere. Keep your head up more and watch the ball longer. When you're close to the net, you can hit the ball down and still have it clear the net. But as you step farther back, the angle changes and it is tougher. Hit the overhead more like your serve and spin it to a corner.

*If Your Overhead Lands Long:* You had no wrist action; you just pushed the ball up. As with the serve, you need to impart wrist action, so hit the overhead like a serve and get some spin on the ball.

*If the ball sails long:* you are probably hitting the ball late. Move your feet more and get behind the ball more so you can step up into the shot. Underjudging the flight pattern of an incoming lob is a universal problem, so step back more than you think you need to, then step up into the shot.

## LOB CORRECTIONS

*If Your Lob Lands Short or in the Net:* Make sure that you give it a little more hit power. A lob is a measurement shot: too little power and the shot will get killed; too much and you miss. You need to develop soft hands to be able to feel and measure the stroke, which must be hit in front of you, dead center, and with enough ball-racquet contact time.

*If Your Lob Lands Long:* You may be feeling too much pressure from the net player and trying to make the lob too good. Again, you must develop the touch to measure this shot.

# FIVE

# COMPETITIVE SYSTEMS TENNIS

In December 1987, Tim Gullikson, one of the top coaches on the pro tour, asked me if I would help him work with Martin Wostenholme, an ATP pro. Our goal was to make Martin a more aggressive player. Tim explained that when he was an ATP player, his coach had taught him a two-zone system: If the ball was in front of the service line on the ground strokes, he would attack; if not, he would stay back behind the baseline. For most players, though, the dividing line was really the imaginary three-quarters line in the service square.

On back-to-back days, Aaron Krickstein was Martin's workout partner. On day one, Aaron's game overshadowed Martin's. But the next day, Martin played more aggressively and beat Aaron. It took me a few weeks to discern the difference. Martin had attacked balls that landed up to nine feet past the service line, and a third zone was born. Once this extra area was added, there were far more balls to attack.

All during the next year I taught three-zone tennis. This particular year Tim was coaching Martina Navratilova. I stayed in close contact, spending a week with them in Oakland, a week in Paris, and a week in New York. I explained to Tim how this new three-zone system was working and suggested that he introduce it to his pupils.

The following December, Tim again asked me to join him, this time in coaching Aaron. Tim's philosophy of play dictated that if a player was pushed far behind the baseline, he should hit a loop-up shot, and zone four was invented. I later added this response to the deep shot hit to either corner. Thus, four-zone tennis was complete.

From all this pro-level work I developed a system of hitting every shot with a reason and purpose. Shortly before I had all the pieces in place on the four-zone system, Ivan Lendl stated that he had finally learned that he didn't have to carry the burden of the point on each shot, though he wasn't explicit about when to go for more and when to remain patient. With my pro friends' help, I devised a system that I call *Competitive Systems Tennis*, a playbook for all levels of the game. Because of it, my game has improved measurably over the past five years. And so will yours as you master this system.

To compete successfully in tennis, as in most sports, you must master certain concepts. In many sports, players are given a playbook to learn. *Competitive Systems Tennis* is your playbook, and I have defined seven areas in which you need to strive for superiority: shot mechanics, play program, conditioning, attitude, state of mind, heart, and guts.

## SHOT MECHANICS

Although I have discussed the shots in great detail, remember that you must always answer the five form questions (see Chapter 3). There are no right or wrong answers to these questions. Each player must tailor the shots to his or her own needs. You can change and experiment on practice days; however, once the match starts, the experimentation must end. If you have answered the mechanics questions, you can rebuild and survive mistakes. Once your form questions are answered, the only two remaining issues are winning the race to the spot and securing the spot (balance).

In addition, before each serve, you must establish the following:

- *Plan*: Whether to serve and volley or stay back, and where to place the serve. In doubles, decide which play to run: poach, fake, or stay (see Chapter 6).

- *Ritual*: To seize control of yourself, calm yourself. Lightly bounce the ball two to four times. Then you must establish a repetitive stance and weight-transfer rhythm pattern.

- *Technique*: Which serve you will hit: five-serve theory or move-the-ball theory.

Before each return of serve, you must establish:

- *Plan*: Whether to return and volley or return and stay back, where your first shot will go (crosscourt, down the line, etc.), and how you want to hit it (topspin or slice).

- *Ritual*: For prepoint participation, follow your weight-transfer rhythm pattern (neutral or one foot in front of the other).

- *Technique*: The five-point form (see Chapter 3).

## PLAY PROGRAM

Having a playing strategy and a playing style will make you a better and more confident player. Every ball played falls into one of three situations, with a corresponding strategy:

## Situation 1: Player Follows Ball to Net Immediately upon Serve or Serve Return

*Following the Serve to Net:* Before the serve is struck, the server plans to approach the net. The server does not examine the results of the serve and then proceed in; it is too late at that point. The first volley is treated as an approach shot: In singles, generally go down the line unless the return is more centered; then crosscourt is equally viable. The second volley is a hard angle hit to the first volley's opposing corner. In doubles, the first volley is treated as an approach shot, which means that it is hit deep crosscourt. The second volley is hit primarily down the line.

*Serve Return and Volley:* The returner has predetermined the tactic of following the ball to the net. The return becomes the approach shot, which should go down the line in singles. The first volley is then angled hard crosscourt. In doubles, the return becomes the approach shot, which goes crosscourt, and the first volley goes down the line.

## Situation 2: Both Players Stay Back.

In this situation, the court is divided into four zones. For every ball landing in one of the zones, the player has a predetermined response.

*Zone 1—The Service Box:* Any ball landing in the service square is an invitation to come to net. The response is a quick, hard, slice approach shot down the line. Shorten the backswing slightly before hitting a quick driving slice with a full follow-through, hard to the corner. If the ball comes back, angle the volley hard crosscourt.

*Zone 2—The Next Nine Feet Past the Service Line:* When the ball lands in this zone, step up from behind the baseline and hit a topspin drive with a two- to four-foot clearance over the net. If the ball lands short or floats into Zone 2, follow the drive in. Even if the ball lands deep in Zone 2, a proficient player can still advance toward the net. If you elect to stay back, fall back behind the base-line.

In Zone 2, the backhand area is divided in half. Hit a step-up run-around forehand in the half adjacent to the court's centerline.

A second form of Zone 2 hitting is called *delay blitz*. When your opponent loops up the shot very high to you, instead of cooperating by letting the ball bounce and push you way back, step up three or four feet into the green zone and crank an overhead or hit a full-blasted ground stroke on the fly.

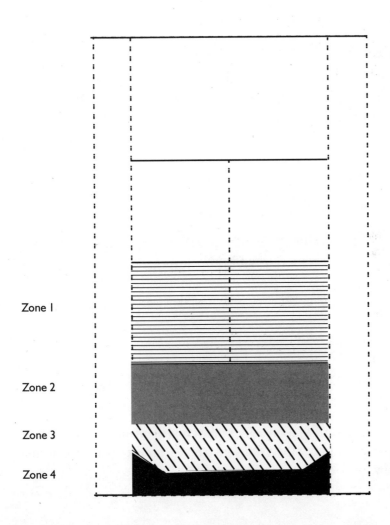

Zone 1

Zone 2

Zone 3

Zone 4

*Zone 3 — The "Patience" Area:* This area is from nine feet beyond the service line to six inches inside the baseline. When the ball lands here, hit a topspin or slice return with a four- to eight- foot clearance over the net to keep your opponent pinned back. Wait for a Zone 1 or 2 ball to fully attack. Do *not* approach the net behind a Zone 3 shot, even after hitting a corner, because of the distance to the five-eighths line. Stopping anywhere short of the five-eighths line opens up both the passing angles and the low balls to your opponent.

*Zone 4 — The Last Six Inches of the Court:* This area includes the six inches in front of the baseline and the deep corner triangle bounded by the baseline and sideline. When the ball lands in the last six inches with good incoming clearance, step back and hit a looped topspin shot with a 10- to 15-foot clearance over the net. If the shot bullets back to the baseline, shorten the start and hit a full follow-through shot, holding ground instead of retreating. Again, do not approach the net.

When the ball lands in the deep corner triangle area, hold the red zone and loop the ball back.

Using a scale with 10 as the maximum power, the appropriate power line for each zone is listed below:

- Zone 1 — 7.5
- Zone 2 — 8.5
- Zone 3 — 7.5
- Zone 4 — 7.5

This four-zone system of tennis creates an aggressive baseline player who patiently awaits a ball to attack. No shot is hit defensively.

## Situation 3: Your Opponent Comes to Net First

The premise in coming to the net is to put physical and mental pressure on the other player. When your opponent comes to the net first, you have five solutions to escape this pressure. Each one is viable if you stay calm:

1. Hit a low shot, making the net player bend.
2. Power the ball right at the player.
3. Pass on the right side of the net player.
4. Pass on the left side of the net player.
5. Lob over the net player.

Master this system to own it. Always trust it, and you will have a strategy to play any player in the world at any level. Once these three situations are mastered, you will always know what kind of shot to hit, where to hit the shot, and where to reposition.

## Styles of Play

You have to define yourself as a player and have a clear game plan before you start. Ideally, you want to develop one of the aggressive game styles so you can win some of your own points.

There are two basic styles of play: *serve (or return) and volley*, and *baseline*. The serve (or returne) and volleyer hits the ball and immediately comes in to net. The baseline style can vary. Brad Gilbert has defined the four kinds of baseline players that he has encountered on the pro tour:

1. *Opportunistic*: A zone player who looks to come in at every opportunity.
2. *Aggressive*: This player steps up into Zone 2 to shorten the court like Agassi, but does not come in. He hits, then retreats to the baseline.

3. *Counterpuncher/Retriever*: A steady player who runs down every ball but doesn't put much on the ball. This player can't *win* a point; she can only watch *you* lose. She keeps the ball in play, hits the ball in the court, and watches the opponent eventually lose the point.

4. *Hard and Steady*: Like Chris Evert, this player keeps the ball in play and moves it around a lot, but all from the backcourt.

Never change a winning game plan. When losing, learn *when* to change a losing strategy. If you're down 4–0 but every game is deuce and you had a few game points, do not change, just get tougher! But if you're down 4–0 and every game is a romp, change plans.

*Defenses:* To defend against the serve and volleyer, hit better returns, low at the volleyer's feet. On second serves and occasionally on first serves, beat the volleyer to the net. To defend against the return and volleyer, hit a wider mix of spins and placement serves. Again, beat the volleyer to the net. To defend against the baseliners:

1. *Opportunistic*: Keep your shots deeper. Be aggressive and come to the net more often to beat this player to the offense. Outsteady your opponent; often the opponent will overhit.

2. *Aggressive*: Come to net more often and keep your shots deep. By not going short, you keep this player pinned back. Outsteady your opponent.

3. *Counterpuncher Retriever*: Bring the zones in two feet and slow down. Once you realize that your opponent cannot win, be patient; don't overhit. It may take 45 more minutes to play, but you won't lose. Hit more middle shots, and bring them in.

4. *Hard and Steady*: Slow down and put more balls in play. Go into the middle of the court more. Move to the net more often. Try some shorter shots to bring this player to the net.

## CONDITIONING

Being better conditioned results in greater stamina and mental well-being. You know you can allow the point to develop because it will not exhaust you. Losing a set is not a big deal, because you have the endurance to play a long match.

Being in condition involves a combination of on-court and off-court activities. On-court, you must play enough sets and do enough drills to build your endurance; off-court, you must prepare yourself physically with a regular program of:

- Diet and weight control. Obviously, a balanced diet is a must. Extra weight makes it tougher to play long matches.
- Weight and nautilus machine work.
- Running, aerobics, steps, etc.
- Stretching.
- Sit-ups, pull-ups, push-ups, etc.

Researchers have established that it's impossible to be in top form physically and mentally 100% of the time. *Periodization* is the ebbing and flowing of your body's performance. You should have periods of less intensive training, building up to maximum as the big matches occur. You must plan for your optimum performance, being careful not to overtrain or leave your best game on the practice field before the match.

## ATTITUDE

"We may be outgunned and outmanned, but we are going to win because we have a superior attitude and state of mind"—Steven Seagal, from *Hard to Kill*.

Believe that you belong on the court and deserve to win the match. Don't moan if your opponent is seeded or you are playing too high up on your team. Go on the court with a businesslike attitude; you are there to win.

Treat your opponent with respect; be respectfully scared. Understand that your opponent came out to win too, so don't treat him or her casually. Play the match at hand with all you have. Don't let your opponent see you sweat; stay emotionally cool. Maintain that arrogance and self-respect throughout the match.

Play one ball at a time, one point at a time. Focus on the positives in your game; don't think of your weaknesses. If you have solid mechanics, a play program and are well-conditioned, you should be bursting with self-esteem and confidence.

## STATE OF MIND

Focus only on the tennis match you are playing. Ignore outside influences; clear your mind of friends, lovers, work, school, and so on. Don't worry about things over which you have no control: wind, sun, scheduling delays, your opponent's clothes. Make yourself comfortable on the court so that your environment never distracts you. Make sure that you have liquids, towels, wristbands, and spare racquets, and that your clothes and shoes fit properly.

During the match watch the ball. Use your form and play programs. Discipline yourself on every point to do these things. Don't just hope it happens; make your body and mind work. Don't be content to do it some of the time; do it all the time. Condition your mind.

## HEART

To be successful, you have to want to win more than your opponent does. Although everyone wants to win, some want to win more than others and will do whatever is required to get that win. Having heart means that you love simply being there; you are willing to put in the time and effort, on and off the court, to give yourself the maximum opportunity to prevail.

When Jim Courier, the 1991 and 1992 French Open Champion, is finished with his match, he often returns to the court to practice with his coach, then goes running. If you want to succeed, you must work at it. The great achievers in any field clearly see what has to be done and gladly do whatever is required. Without heart — without that love of the endeavor itself — you will not find the discipline necessary to do the work.

## GUTS

Having guts is the ability to be tough not just some of the time, but all the time. Guts enable you to get tougher when the match gets tougher. Guts give you the courage to go out and play aggressively with courage and conviction. Guts sustain you when a long, hard-fought match is almost over and you need to reach inside yourself for an even higher level of participation. Guts enable you to perform despite adverse conditions, to ignore all obstacles real or imagined, to practice until something is mastered completely, not just halfway.

Sometimes tennis necessitates a great deal of work. If you don't have the courage to rise to that challenge, you will fall short of the goal of being a great player.

Remember, you must master all seven areas to play with the degree of consistency needed to be a winning competitor. Once you master these seven areas, you'll find it easier to assuage your nervousness, go out on the court, and stay loose, and perform at your highest level.

# SIX

# DOUBLES PLAY

**M**any tennis leagues that people participate in are doubles leagues. So in addition to basic tennis strategy, you should be familiar with doubles strategy.

## CHARGE THE NET

In high-level tennis, the goal in doubles is to reach the net before the other team does. The server rushes the net on the serve, and the returner rushes the net on the serve return. The team that controls the net usually wins.

Now the first reality sets in: The serve may be so strong that the returner cannot follow the return to the net. Thus, if the serving team is good at the net, holding or winning the serving games becomes easier. The second reality is that most inexperienced players don't have a strong serve. When they follow it to the net, they lose. The third reality is that beginners are usually weak in their volleying skills, so being at the net often offers no great advantage.

Although your ultimate goal is to learn to come in, you can get away with staying back if your opponents also stay back or are unable to hit effective volleys.

## DEEP TO DEEP; CLOSE TO CLOSE

Whether you are coming in or staying back, the basic rule of doubles is to hit your balls *deep to deep* and *close to close*. The close line is the five-eighths line, discussed earlier (see Chapter 3). If you are not in this close, aim for the deep target, because if you give the net person too many feet to see the ball coming, he will be able to handle it easily (assuming that the net person has some skills). In other words, if you are deep in the court, hit deep, which is usually crosscourt in doubles.

When you are close to the net (five-eighths line or closer), your target is close. Aim your shot around the opposite close person, even if she is the better player, because she has fewer seconds and less footage to react. The second choice is to short-angle the deep person.

## TEAMWORK

Doubles can be lots of fun. There are two people on each side of the court, and they must know how to work together. In doubles there are many situations in which the team must move together as a unit or learn to help each other. Basically, each player is responsible for half the court, but good teams learn what each person is capable of covering and do whatever is necessary to work the court well together.

Being a good singles player does not necessarily make you a good doubles partner. You must have the proper attitude about your role and a respect for your partner's. Your attitude must be that you want every ball to come to you and are anticipating that the shot will be hit to you. This is not an insult to your partner, who has the same attitude. If you are not expecting the ball to come to you, you are going to get caught napping. You're partner will be forced to take many shots that could and should be yours. Even when your partner has better skills, you must still be an eager participant.

It is both partners' job to keep the team pumped up. If you act or believe that your partner is beneath you, that you do not want to be on the same court with this person, then *you* are a lousy partner and will lose. A college coach had a top player who repeatedly asked for new partners. After the third request, the coach told his player, "You are clearly the better player, but you are out of the doubles lineup, since you cannot work with any of your teammates."

On Sundays I usually play mixed doubles with my wife and another couple. One day I remarked that the other man's game was much better when we were partners than when he was partnered with one of our wives. His response was, "When I play with you I know you will be in the right place and not miss, so I can concentrate on my game. When I just worry about me I can play very well." That was a brilliant observation. When all your energy is focused on your partner, you waste your abilities. The best you can do is focus on your game; the more you focus on your partner, the worse your play will be.

There are three things that make a good doubles team: a prematch game plan, game plan adjustments based on your opponent's play, and between-point huddles. First you must discuss your game plan before the match. Included in this discussion is how to handle certain situations: Who will take the shot in the middle? Who covers the lobs? Many players, including some pros, like to see how the opponent plays first and then develop a game plan. This is nonsense. I want you to have a San Francisco Forty-Niner tennis mentality. The Forty-Niners have their first 25 plays scripted and take their game to the opponent. Only if your opponent stops you cold do you come off your plan. There is a huge difference between being a controller and a reactor.

Second, during the match, you are to determine what is working for your team and what patterns you see in the opposition. By the third game you should have a full scouting report on your opponents—their forehands, backhands, serves, volleys, and overheads. Good teams adjust their game plan as they see their opponents play. Good partners are receptive to information gleaned from these patterns. If your partner tells you to move wide on the serve return because the serves are all going to that side, your response should be, "Good pickup partner!" Good teams adjust together. Bad teams don't talk or help each other.

The third aspect of a good doubles team is taking the time after each point to momentarily huddle. I call these *formula huddles*. On the serve side, you might say, "The formula is first serve in and net person be active." On the serve return side, the formula is to call your return (for example, crosscourt, slice) and tell your partner whether you are coming in or staying back. Since you have only 25 seconds between the points, the huddle should be quick; it is simply a reconfirmation of the game-plan commitment.

## MOVING ON THE COURT

As soon as you achieve any level of competence at the net in doubles as the server's partner, you should be actively moving — called *poaching* — across the court to intercept the ball. The purpose of the net person's movement is to prevent the returner from seeing the same formation all the time.

There are three ways for teams to determine movement on the serve:

1. The net person may move spontaneously and the back person has to read his partner and quickly react. I don't like this system because it pulls the server's attention off the job of serving and adds another — watching his partner.

2. During the huddle, the players agree how to move and cover the court.

3. The net player hand signals the server on each serve, and the server verbally acknowledges the signal. This is the system I use. By deciding the play movement before the serve is struck, both players have a designated job to do, so all they have to do is focus on themselves.

### The Poach Play

On this play, the net player waits until the serve has landed and just prior to the return, sprints across the court toward the net on the diagonal so as to cut the angle off the returner's ball. If the server is

The closed fist tells your partner that you are going to stay

coming to the net, he takes 2 or 3 steps forward and then sprints to the opposite side of the court. If the server stays back, he should hold the serve position for 1 second, and then sprint along the baseline to the other side of the court. On the poach play, the server does the fake.

## The Fake Play

Just before the serve lands, the net person runs 2 steps as if he is going to poach, but stops and quickly returns to the original position.

Two fingers down mean that you are going to fake a poach; this
is important to tell your partner so that you fake only the
opponents, not your partner

The server will either come in immediately or stay back—on both
the poach and the fake play, the net player intercepts the serve return and puts the ball away. With the net player moving so often
and unpredictably, your opponents will be distracted and hopefully
miss many returns. The third option is to stay in the original
positions.

Once the point has begun, the net player may still poach. This
is done spontaneously. Whenever the player at the net sees a good
opportunity to get a ball that is struck toward his partner, the net
player should be active and poach.

An open hand means you are going to poach

## WATCHING THE BALL

Should you look back when your partner hits the ball? In singles it is obvious that you must follow the ball at all times, but in doubles there is some controversy about this. Within a three-month period, one of the major tennis magazines presented opposing opinions on this, complete with tips on what to do. You should definitely not look back when your partner is serving; there is no need to see where the ball is going because it has to go in the service square or the point won't be played.

The rest of the time, however, there is no guaranteed placement of your partner's shot, so you want to glimpse back over your shoulder to see where the ball has been hit. This gives you a better chance of reacting to what happens next and helps your concentration, just as it does in singles.

# SEVEN

# THE
# MENTAL
# GAME

The mental side of the game is just as important as the physical side. No matter how good your strokes or how well-conditioned you are, if you don't have the mental strength to fight and survive, you will not win. When teaching the mental aspects of the game, I discuss four areas: effort, focus, discipline, and attitude.

## EFFORT

No player misses on purpose; every player thinks that he is trying very hard, but some players do not realize the amount of effort required. Charles Barkley, the basketball superstar, recently accused one of his teammates of not trying. Yet, if you asked his teammate about it, he would say that he was trying as hard as possible. Obviously there is a difference in semantics as to what it means to "try." In tennis there are three things you must do when you "try":

1. Move your feet *before* the point starts. By moving your feet before the point begins, you show that you are ready, you have good intensity, and your body language is positive — even arrogant. You announce that you are ready to play.

2. Move your feet *during* the point. By moving your feet during the point, you assume that the opponent's shot is going to be hit into the court, and you are prepared to run it down.

3. Hit your shots with purpose. When a player first starts to play tennis, the only concern is to hit the ball over the net anywhere. However, as a player advances and learns play strategy, making an effort to execute that strategy is critical. My standard question to the player is, "If you can't control yourself, how can you expect to win?" And the key element to controlling yourself (and your shots) is attitude — specifically, self-respect. As the opponent's ball comes toward you, you must use your form and play program, no matter how tough the shot seems. You must have a "can do" attitude.

A common problem is that players *try* too hard. Part of the mental game is for each player to try to make the opponent think that he isn't good enough to win the match. The player who buys into that pressure will be the loser. If, before you begin to play, you believe that your skills are not going to be up to the task, the match is already over. The key is to play confidently *within your skill and knowledge level*. Don't get baited into believing that you must try to exceed your capabilities.

Don't try to hit *great* shots with *great* depth and *great* placement. If you do, you are trying too hard and will fail too often. Go for *good* shots with *good* depth and *good* placement. The key mental trick to staying positive about your skills is to make your quality judgment based on your hit, not your opponent's response. If you wait until you see how your opponent handles your shot before you make your positive judgment, you are going to be unhappy most of the time. Don't get caught up in the feeling that if your opponent hits the ball back, your shot must not have been that good. If you do, you will end up trying too hard.

# FOCUS

The second area of mental toughness is focus, and the key to focus is concentration. At the 1991 French Open, one of the top men's coaches told me that he believes that it is impossible for any player to maintain his concentration for five full sets — and he's doubtful about three sets. The mind does have a tendency to drift off, so how can a player maintain focus?

In tennis, concentration involves both a big-picture and a little-picture aspect. The big picture is that the player must concentrate throughout the entire match — sometimes for three straight hours. The little picture is that on each shot, one ball at a time, the player has to watch the ball and focus on where to hit it.

During the actual play time, the most important mental task is to stay focused in the present. My wife was a world-class gymnast as a youth. She has told me that in her sport, one always focuses on the next move while doing the present move. Unfortunately, in tennis this leads to disaster. When a player thinks about the future before completing the present task, this results in two mistakes: (1) not watching the ball — because the player's head has come up to see the great shot she is going to hit, and (2) abandoning form part way through the stroke — because the player is busy trying to reposition for the next shot. In tennis, a checklist approach is best: Know what the next task is, but do one task at a time and finish it completely before going on to the next one.

Maintaining your concentration in the present also applies to not making judgments about your last shot. A player may be so happy about the great shot she hit that she forgets to play the rest of the point. The opposite also occurs: A player is so upset by a poor shot that the point is abandoned. The last shot is history; get yourself into the present.

Besides learning to hold your concentration during the point, you must also learn to hold your concentration between points. Only 25% of the time is actually spent hitting the ball; the rest is in between points. It is easy to sightsee between points, watching people on the next court or people walking by. The best thing to do is to look at your strings and tell yourself how well you plan to play the next point.

Establishing patterns of behavior is a good way to maintain focus. Every player should have an unvarying ritual of preparation before serving and returning serve. John McEnroe compared hitting a serve to shooting a basketball free throw: No one is in the way to guard you, and there is lots of time to shoot. In any poor serving performance, including at the pro level, rushing is the big problem. Therefore, your ritual of preparation should be designed to slow you down and relax you before every serve. Bounce the ball a few times, breathe deeply, and focus on what you intend to do. If you miss your first serve, take at least three seconds to recompose yourself and go through the ritual again.

On serve return, follow your ritual pattern. Based on the speed and spin of the serve, you may need to vary your position, but not the ritual. As stated in Chapter 3, the key is to have an early prehit preparation of foot movement and stepping forward.

After missing a shot or losing a game, maintaining concentration can be very difficult unless you can learn to bury the failure. When you miss a shot, you must forget it immediately. When you lose a game, forget it. If you harp on it, you are not playing present-tense tennis. When players berate themselves for a minor failure, they start a negative cycle of failure. The more a player misses, the more upset and worried he becomes; the more upset and worried he becomes, the more he misses. When you miss, take a practice swing and remind yourself in a positive manner what the shot is supposed to be. Close your eyes and visualize the shot being executed sucessfully. A player must be mentally tough enough not to believe that one mistake makes him a failure. Any miss or loss must be perceived as an aberration.

## DISCIPLINE

The third area of mental preparedness is the discipline of execution. When players are trying and concentrating but still missing, what's wrong? The problem is probably a lack of discipline of execution.

The key to playing mentally tough tennis is to discipline your-self to use the knowledge you currently have. In most cases, players are playing other players who are at the same skill level or a little better or worse. Therefore, the player who performs at his knowl-edge level is going to be the winner. The job at hand on each and every ball is to not panic, to stay in control of your mind and emotions, and to execute the shot as you have learned it.

One often hears of players who are great in practice but cannot perform under pressure. The key to performance is the discipline of execution. Think of your match as just one more practice day and make it an extension of your practice. You should be playing the way you practice and practicing the way you plan to play. When I play, I don't think about winning or losing. I know that I have good shots and an excellent play program, so I use my knowledge and skills and let winning take care of itself. When you play to win, you put too much pressure on yourself. Worse is to play not to lose — then you play scared and tight. You must trust yourself to do the best you can. When I play I never go for winners; I hit each shot with a purpose. I put no extra emotional stake or energy into any one shot.

## ATTITUDE

The last aspect of mental toughness is how to make yourself a win-ner. And the answer is attitude. First, both winning and losing are contagious. For example, when the score is 4 to 4, one team may be thinking, we'll win because we've won our last three matches. The other team may be thinking, we'll lose because we always fall short. Which team is more likely to win? Winning and losing are attitudes, and winning attitudes produce winners.

It is important that you get some wins in practice, so that when you compete you see yourself as a winner. Visualize yourself as a winner before you play. When you walk on the court, you have to see yourself as a player who deserves to win the match.

# WINNING THE MENTAL GAME

When you play a match, you must be mentally ready. Serious match play requires serious preparation. You need to know your needs and comfort levels and cater to them. You should have two identical racquets that have been recently strung. Your clothes and shoes should fit properly. If you like liquids, towels, and wristbands, have them. If you feel ill at ease, you will be mentally distracted and fail for certain. You need to come to the court with a clear head. You cannot be thinking about school, your job, your next appointment, friends, or parents. You need to be mentally ready to do battle with your tennis opponent.

When you play you must treat your opponent with respect, understanding that he or she is capable of winning the match. If you treat your opponent lightly, he may get so much momentum built up that you cannot save the match. If you are having an easy time, set tougher goals for yourself during the match to ensure your continued focus. Try to hold your opponent to no games or under a certain point total. Sometimes the opponent just has a bad start; if you let down and assume that the match is going to be a cakewalk, the tables can quickly be turned.

Finishing off games, sets, and matches in which you are ahead is the biggest mental skill there is. First, it is important that you have the correct goal: You are not playing to win, but you expect that through your excellent execution you will produce a victory. Thus, you must step onto the court with a vision of yourself being successful. Too many players just try to make a good showing. If that is your goal, that is all you will get. Second, when you are winning, your opponent has two choices: (1) give up and believe that you are the superior player, or (2) get tougher. You must prepare for the onslaught of his increased effort. If he cannot do this, you will win easily. If he can raise the level of his game, you will be ready for him.

A few years ago, one of the touring pros lost a match in which she had two match points (one more point and she would have won). She said that if she had been down instead of up, she would have won. The lesson here is that being down, she knew she had to battle; being up, she forgot. The mental trick to play on yourself is to pretend you are down no matter what the score is. Pretend that unless you start to battle a little more you will lose — so you'd better get in gear and stay there.

# EIGHT

## HOW TO IMPROVE YOUR GAME

Tennis is a very rewarding game. On television, the pros make it look easy, but in reality, tennis is a difficult game to learn. This is part of what makes it so rewarding to achieve some measure of success. Receiving good instruction and being patient with yourself are the keys to improvement.

### PRIVATE COACHING

There are two professional tennis teaching organizations: the United States Professional Teaching Registry (USPTR) and the United States Professional Teaching Association (USPTA). Membership in these organizations indicates that a pro has passed a minimum test of competence but does not guarantee quality instruction. Realize that your needs vary depending on your level and ability.

Some pros are excellent with beginners, but that's all. Other are excellent at the high end of the game, but have no patience with beginners.

In general, there are four things to look for when seeking an instructor. First, the instructor should have a level of competence in the game. The most effective teachers are those who teach what they know. Next, the instructor should be a good teacher and communicator who cares about your progress and has the flexibility to work with you as an individual. Third, your instructor should behave as if running a business — beginning and ending the lessons on time shows respect for you and your time. Last, your instructor should be current. The game is ever-changing, so to remain on top of the game, the instructor should be entering tournaments and playing competitively as well as attending the pro tournaments.

For older children and beginning adults, group tennis lessons are an excellent and economical way to begin. Look for a program that has a structure of advancement and a good student-teacher ratio. I never teach more than eight students at a time.

## WATCHING TENNIS

One of the best ways to learn tennis is to watch tennis. There is an entire learning process called *visualization*. Sybervision has made many films of correct tennis form, and there are numerous tennis videos you can watch.

You can learn an incredible amount from watching the pros. I attend at least three major pro tournaments a year and learn something every time I go. Television offers an excellent opportunity to watch the professional players in action, all from the comfort of your own living room. Invite your practice partner over and discuss what you observe.

Throughout the year both the men's and women's pro tours continue all across the world, and many of their tournaments are televised.

The most important are the four Grand Slam events: the Australian Open is played in Melbourne in January on a hard surface; the French Open is played in Paris in May on red clay; Wimbledon is played in London in July on grass; and the U.S. Open is played in New York in September on hard courts.

Each surface causes the ball to bounce differently, thus changing the skill emphasis needed to win. Clay is a slow court surface that grabs the ball and slows it down, so a good backcourt game and lots of endurance are necessary for success. Chris Evert's game was ideal for this type of surface. Grass is the fastest surface. Since the ball skids off the court quickly, speed, power, and a great net game are required. Boris Becker and Stephan Edberg excel on grass. The hard-court surface is somewhere in between clay and grass, so the all-court game is important. There is a wide variation of speed on the hard courts, depending on the amount of sand mixed in with the pavement surface. The more sand, the more grab, and the slower the court.

In 1988, the Olympics added tennis as a medal sport, indicating the increasing prestige and interest in this sport.


## READING

There are many good tennis books written to help players at all stages of the game. Some people learn best when seeing the words written out. All libraries and bookstores have a wide selection from which to choose.


## ATTAINING SENSUAL AWARENESS

One of the keys to learning about tennis is to be sensually aware of your body. Without looking back or down, you must be aware of where your racquet is and where your arms legs, knees, head, and eyes are. You must develop a feel for these parts. Many years ago during the Zen heydays, teachers stressed sensual awareness, though it is just as relevant today as it was then. A good way to increase sensual awareness is to practice swinging the racquet off the court. This helps acquaint your body with the racquet.

# PRACTICING

If you want to improve, you must practice. A good work week might include one lesson and three hitting times. You can use the backboard or a ball machine to practice a particular shot. The problem with these methods is that you are not experiencing live hitting.

If you practice with someone of lesser ability, you can work on aspects of your game without the pressure of success. You get to see the ball leave someone's racquet, which is critical in learning to react. If you practice with someone of equal ability, you are pushed to perform. If you practice with someone better than you, you are challenged to play your best. The more you can play up, the faster you will reach that level. Playing down boosts your confidence; playing up pushes your development. A balance is critical.

A mistake many players make is that they only play games. Everyone needs some drill work to gain control of their shots. On your strokes and volleys, it is productive to work in target zones with your partner. For instance, both of you aim your shots crosscourt or down the line. If you change segments every five minutes — doing both crosscourts and down the lines and then repeating the process at the net — you have a 40-minute workout.

For the serve, find a partner to work on serve and serve return. Each takes turns serving and returning. The year that Bjorn Borg won his first Wimbledon title, he worked for two hours a day, two weeks straight, just on his serve. Matts Wilander, after winning his U.S. Open semi-finals match, went home and worked on his serve into the night. The next day he made 42 great first serves in a row — the equivalent of throwing 42 straight strikes in baseball — and won the tournament. That's what practice does!

## Drill Games

*Segment Scoring:* One player serves until one of the players reaches 10 points. This helps you focus on every point and gets you used to long games. You can add handicap scoring to prepare yourself for the "come-from-behind win": For example, your opponent starts with a score of five and you have to play catch-up.

Another way to handicap the score is by playing the no ad system. There is a sliding scale of point production: Player A starts the first game ahead 2 points to 0 points. If player B wins that game, player A starts game two 3 points to 0. If player A wins the second game, the handicap slides back down to two points for game three.

Another way to handicap the game is to give player A five free points to be used at her discretion. Any time player A needs a point she can draw from her free-point bag. Here the player learns when to distinguish significant points or opportunities.

Try playing with both the first and second serves. In order for the better player to score, he must win both points. The lesser player scores every time he wins a point, and I give a bonus point to the lesser player for winning both serves. Thus the lesser player can score three points in each segment, and the better player only one.

## COMPETING

After you have reached a certain level of competence, the fastest manner to promote growth is to compete. For both children and adults, there are leagues and tournaments at all levels, from the lowest to the highest. Find a level to compete and climb the tennis ladder.

Most leagues and tournaments are organized on the tier system. For your own enjoyment and that of others, it is important that you play at or near the real level of your game. The purpose of competing is to improve. If you play at a level way below your game, you get bored and have no fun. If you play too far above your game you cannot handle the skill level.

For children, all states have competitive tournaments year-round, and some states have tiers of play. There are summer leagues sponsored by the United States Tennis Association (USTA). All high schools and some junior high schools have team programs in tennis.

For adults, all states have local tennis organizations that sponsor competitive tournament-level play. Many states run league programs during the day, night, and on weekends. Many of these leagues are tiered by the new USTA rating system (see below). The USTA itself runs a summer league at a multitier level, which culminates in a national championship.

For families, many states run different combinations of family-member tournaments. During the summer, the Equitable Insurance Company sponsors a family tournament in which the regional winners compete at the U.S. Open in New York.

If you join a tennis club or organization, there will be many competitive and social activities to help you improve your tennis game; you do not have to join a private club to do this. Many recreation districts have tennis clubs that run programs. Call around; there's a tennis program out there just waiting for you!

The United States Tennis Association has devised the following player-rating system:

**1.0** This player is just starting to play tennis.

**1.5** This player has limited experience and is still working primarily on getting the ball in play.

**2.0** This player needs on-court experience. This player has obvious stroke weaknesses but is familiar with basic positions for singles and doubles play.

**2.5** This player is learning to judge where the ball is going, although court coverage is weak. This player can sustain a rally of slow pace with other players of the same ability.

**3.0** This player is consistent when hitting medium-paced shots but is not comfortable with all strokes and lacks control when trying for directional intent, depth, or power.

**3.5** This player has achieved improved stroke dependability and direction on moderate shots, but still lacks depth and variety. This player is starting to exhibit more aggressive net play, has improved court coverage, and is developing teamwork in doubles.

**4.0**    This player has dependable strokes, including directional intent and depth on both forehand and backhand sides on moderate shots, plus the ability to use lobs, overheads, approach shots, and volleys with some success. This player occasionally forces errors when serving, and teamwork in doubles is evident.

**4.5**    This player has begun to master the use of power and spins and is beginning to handle pace, has sound footwork, can control depth of shots, and is beginning to vary tactics according to opponents. This player can hit first serves with power and accuracy and place the second serve and is able to rush the net successfully.

**5.0**    This player has good shot anticipation and frequently has an outstanding shot or exceptional consistency around which a game may be structured. This player can regularly hit winners or force errors off short balls and can put away volleys; can successfully execute lobs, drop shots, half volleys, and overhead smashes; and has good depth and spin on most second serves.

**5.5**    This player has developed power and/or consistency as a major weapon. This player can vary strategies and styles of play in a competitive situation and hits dependable shots in stress situations.

**6.0–7.0**    These players will generally not need NTRP ratings. Past or present rankings will speak for themselves. The 6.0 player typically has had intensive training for national tournament competition at the junior and collegiate levels and has obtained a sectional and/or national ranking. The 6.5 player has a reasonable chance of succeeding at the 7.0 level and has extensive satellite tournament experience. The 7.0 is a world-class player who is committed to tournament competition on the international level and whose major source of income is tournament prize winnings.

# CONDITIONING AND EXERCISING

Tennis is a sport for which you must develop long-term conditioning and speed-burst conditioning. Entire books have been written on conditioning, and there are many videos to follow. ESPN often has two hours a day of fitness and conditioning programs that you can watch at home. But be sure to talk to your doctor before beginning any exercise program.

For long-term conditioning, running or walking distances is the first choice, either outside or on a treadmill. Aerobics classes and the steppers and climbers that many health clubs have are great ways to condition your body, and so is the bicycle — either exercise or regular. You should also work with weights — both on the machines and with free weights.

In tennis, the first step is critical when running to the ball. You must work off the court to develop the necessary acceleration. Straight sprint work is the best way to do this. An All-American basketball player I know likes to alternate long run days with sprint days. Resistance running is also good. There is a toy you can buy that is like a harness: As you run, a friend holds the toy, which resists your movement. A cheap replacement is to use a big bath towel. I like to use a quick movement routine around my driveway in which I alternate sprints and side steps. Jumping rope is also good for developing quick feet.

Stretching has become important in all sports. Stretching both before and after exercise helps warm you up and cool you down, minimizing the chance of injury. Always stretch your ankles and Achilles area, legs, arms, neck, and shoulders:

- For your Achilles tendons, place one foot about two to three feet in front of the other and press the back one against a wall or fence. Hold for 20 seconds, then change legs. Repeat four or five times.

- Hold on to a fence or net post for support and lift one leg slightly and rotate your ankle 10 times clockwise, then 10 times counterclockwise. Turn and change legs.

- Circle your shoulders forward 10 times, then reverse. This exercise should be done slowly and gently.

- To relax and stretch your neck, touch your chin to chest, then try to touch your right ear to your right shoulder, then drop your head back, then try to touch your left ear to your left shoulder. Reverse. Repeat five times in each direction.

- To stretch your arms, place your right arm straight in front of you at shoulder level, then grab the triceps area with your left hand, gently pulling the right arm toward your left side. Hold ten seconds. Reverse. Repeat each side four more times.

The surest way to sustain an injury is to play without first warming up properly. During the warm-up, you are trying to slowly warm up your muscles so they will be able to perform properly. The first step is to actually stay warm. If your muscles are cold and you attempt quick moves, you increase your chance for injury. On cool days, make sure you dress warmly.

To minimize injury and maximize your potential for success, you should follow this ritual: Start with a prematch stretch, then take shadow swings with your racquet. Practice all your shots, achieving a comfort level before you play.

During the actual match warm-up, ready your shots for play. Start slowly and gradually increase to game-speed stroking. Warm up all your shots and try to stay calm. If you are experiencing difficulty with your shots, hang in there. Focus on the ball; stay confident and upbeat.

Own the materials presented; trust the materials presented; use the materials presented; relax, have a good time, and Enjoy this great game of tennis.

# INDEX